Linwood, Macton, and Erbsville Ontario in Colour Photos, Saving Our History One Photo at a Time

Photography
by Barbara Raué
2014

Series Name:
Cruising Ontario

Book 73: Linwood and Area

Cover photo: 5186 Ament Line, Linwood

Series Name: Cruising Ontario
Saving Our History One Photo at a Time

Other Books by Barbara Raue

Coins of Gold

Arrows, Indians and Love

The Life and Times of Barbara
Volume 1: Inventions That Have Enhanced My Life
Volume 2: Entertainment That I Have Enjoyed
Volume 3: East Coast Trips
Volume 4: Olympics Have Always Intrigued Me
Volume 5: Wonders of the World
Volume 6: Caribbean Cruises We Have Enjoyed
Volume 7: Animals
Volume 8: Storms and Other Major Disasters in My Lifetime
Volume 9: Wars, Terrorist Attacks and Major Disasters

The Cromwell Family Book

Laura Secord Discovered

Visit Barbara's website to view all of her books
http://barbararaue.ca

The Township of Wellesley is the rural, north-western township of the Regional Municipality of Waterloo. The township comprises the communities of Bamberg, Crosshill, Hawkesville, Heidelberg, Kingwood, Knight's Corners, Linwood, Macton, St. Clements, Wallenstein and Wellesley.

The country scenery and rolling hills, along with its small town feel, have transformed the township into a commuter town with the population travelling into the nearby cities of Kitchener and Waterloo for work.

Wellesley Township was surveyed in 1842, but settlers were in this area long before. The town of Wellesley's original name was *Schmidtsville*, derived from its founding settler, John Schmidt. In 1851, the town was renamed *Wellesley* after Richard Wellesley, 1st Marquess Wellesley, the eldest brother of Arthur Wellesley, 1st Duke of Wellington. The community quickly grew to be the largest economic centre in rural Waterloo Region with a wood mill, feed mill, grain mill (which still stands after being constructed in 1856), leather tanner, cheese factory, restaurants and housing, and many other businesses that also brought much trade to the town from the nearby farms and farming villages.

When the Waterloo County boundaries were established in 1852 they included the townships of Waterloo, Wellesley, Wilmot, Woolwich, and North Dumfries.

The first library in Wellesley Village was incorporated in 1900. The current branch is located in the former S.S. No. 16 Wellesley Township public school building. The school closed its doors in 1967.

Macton

Macton is on the northern boundary line of Wellesley Township, three miles northeast of Linwood, twenty miles northwest of Berlin, three miles east of Wallenstein. Macton was settled later than St. Clements, mostly by Irish people.

Erbsville

Erbsville is located about five miles west of Kitchener.

Table of Contents

Linwood

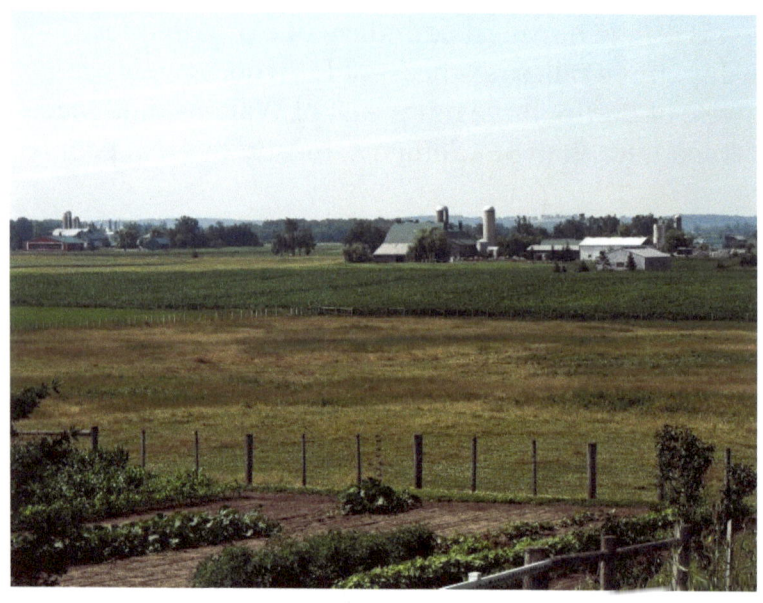

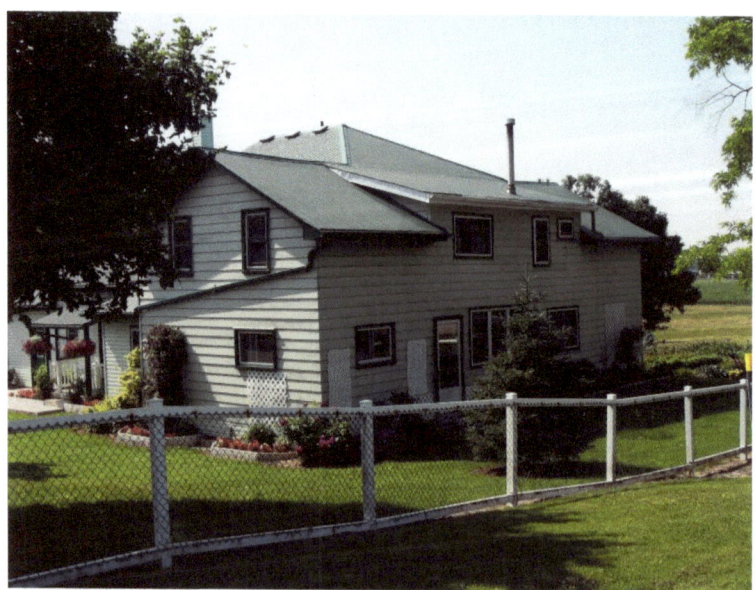

4477 Ament Line

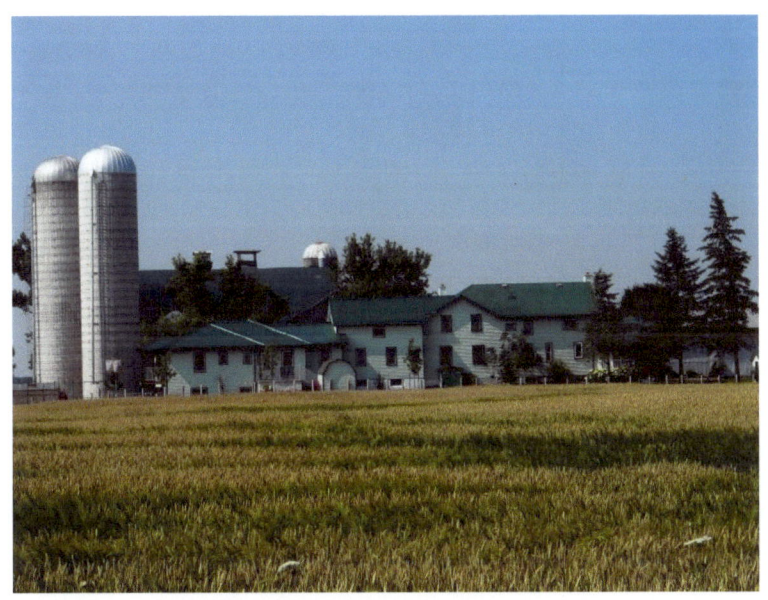

Mennonite farms

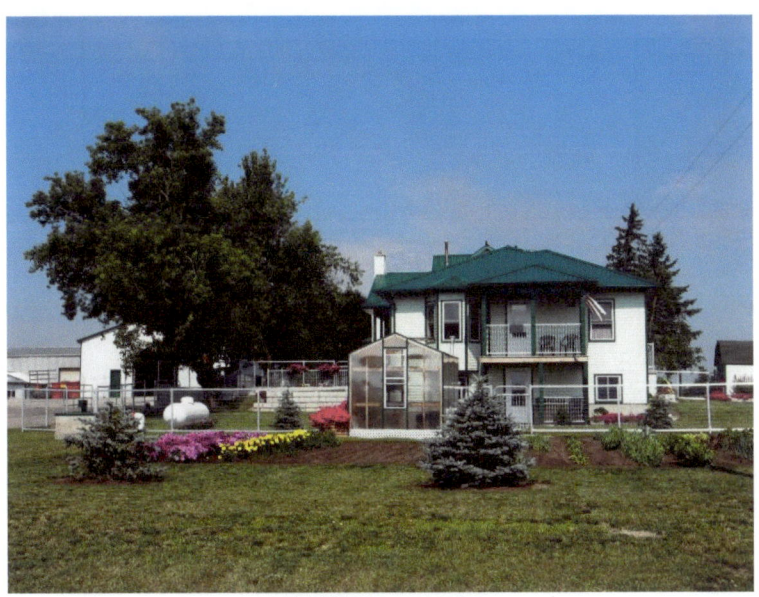

4250 Ament Line

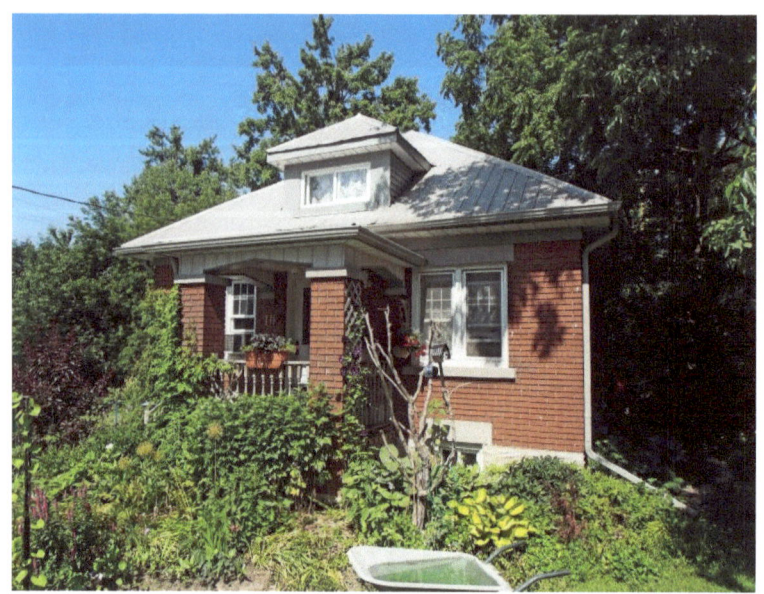

1030 Ament Line – Italianate, hip roof, dormer

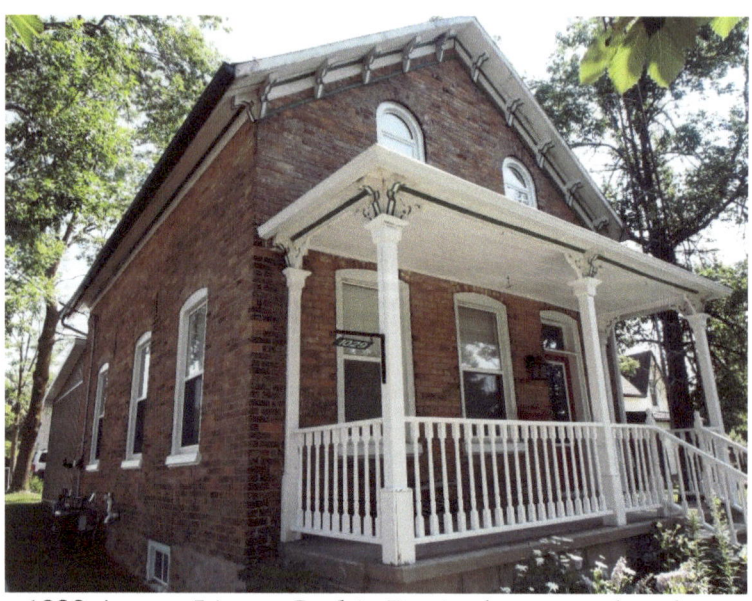

1029 Ament Line – Gothic Revival, cornice brackets

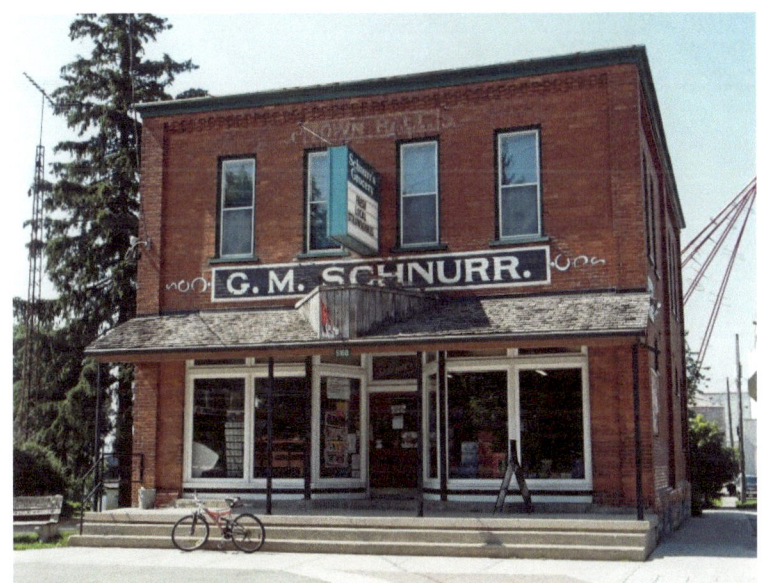

5168 Ament Line – dentil moulding

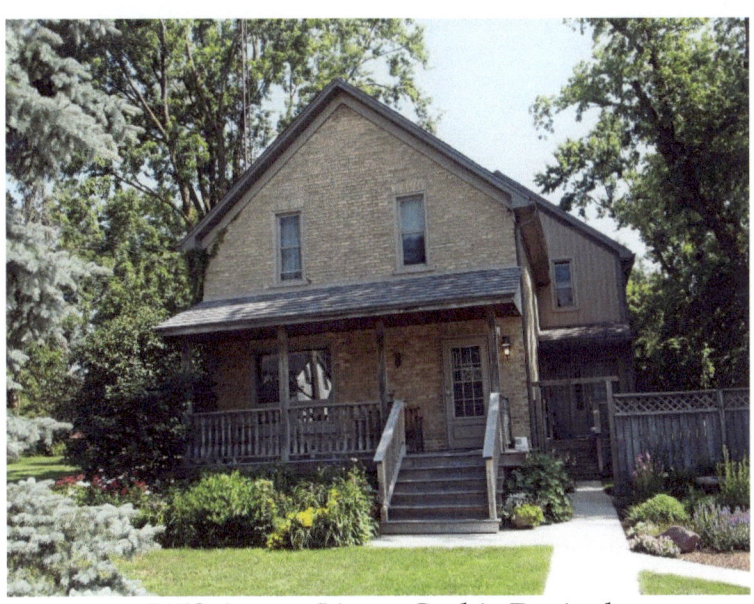

5159 Ament Line – Gothic Revival

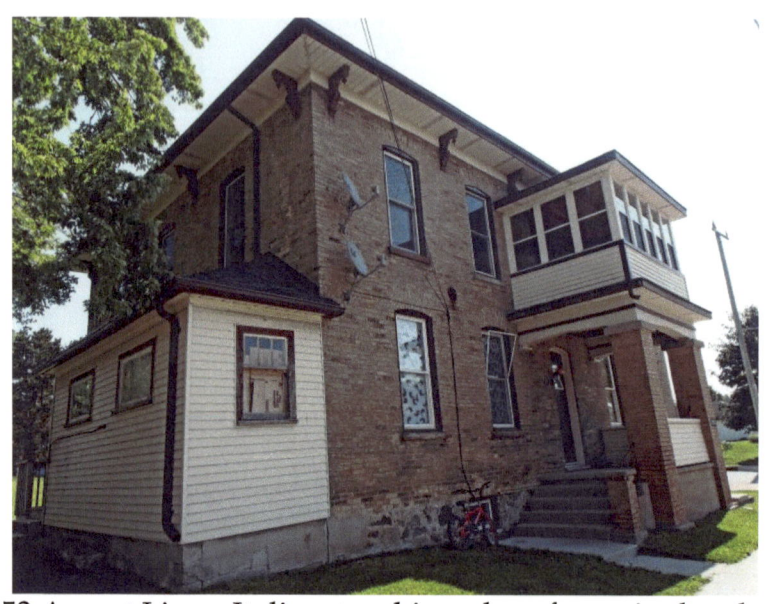

5153 Ament Line – Italianate – hipped roof, cornice brackets, Cobblestone basement wall

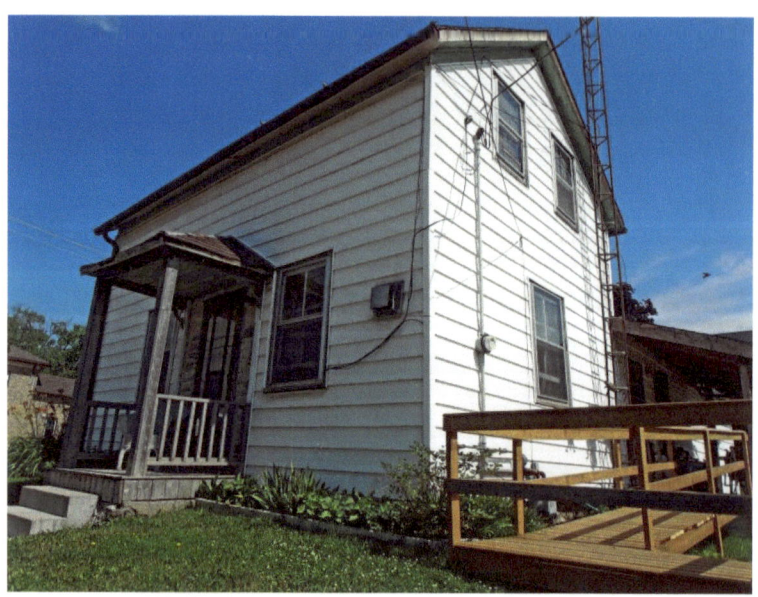

5145 Ament Line – Gothic Revival

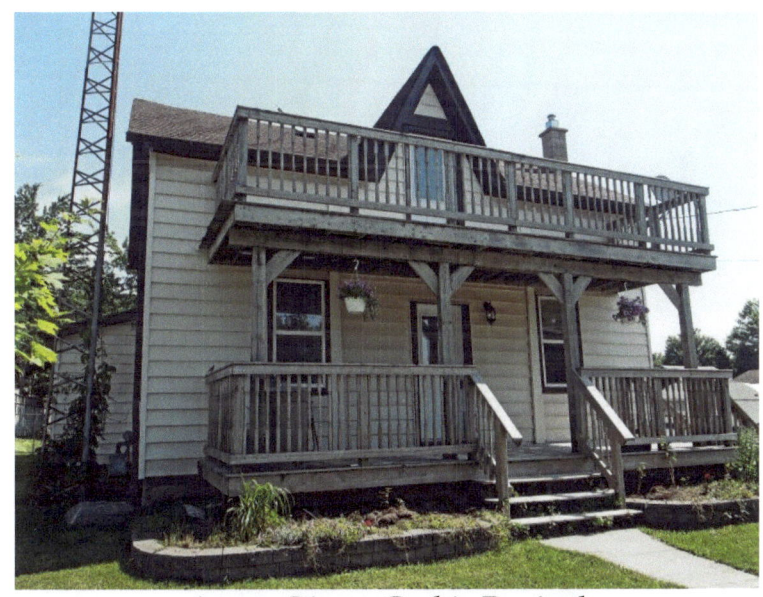

Ament Line – Gothic Revival

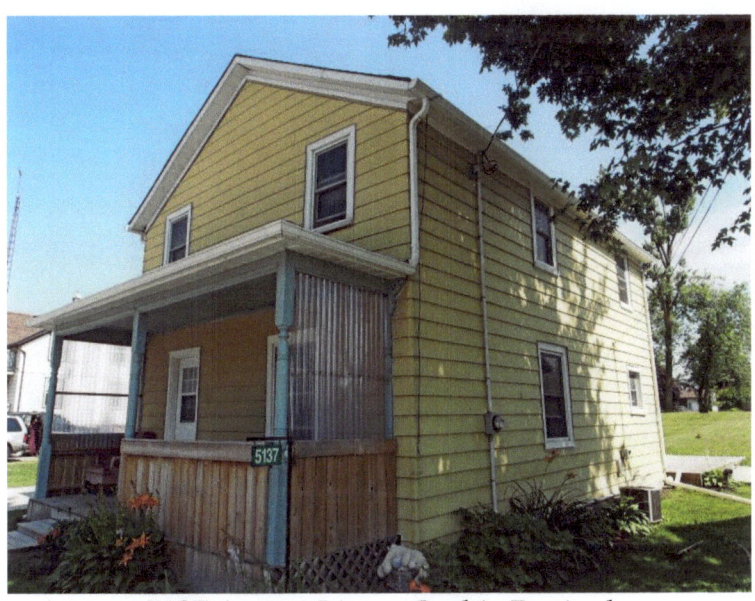

5137 Ament Line – Gothic Revival

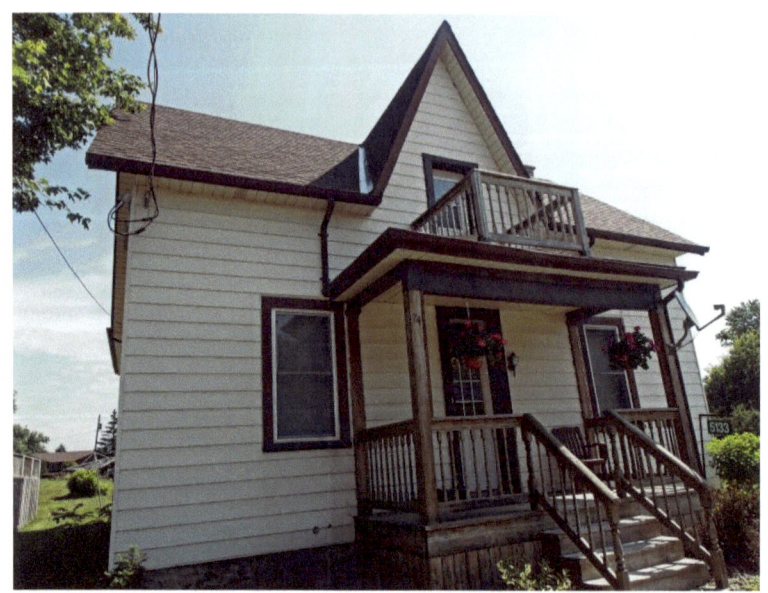

5133 Ament Line – Gothic Revival

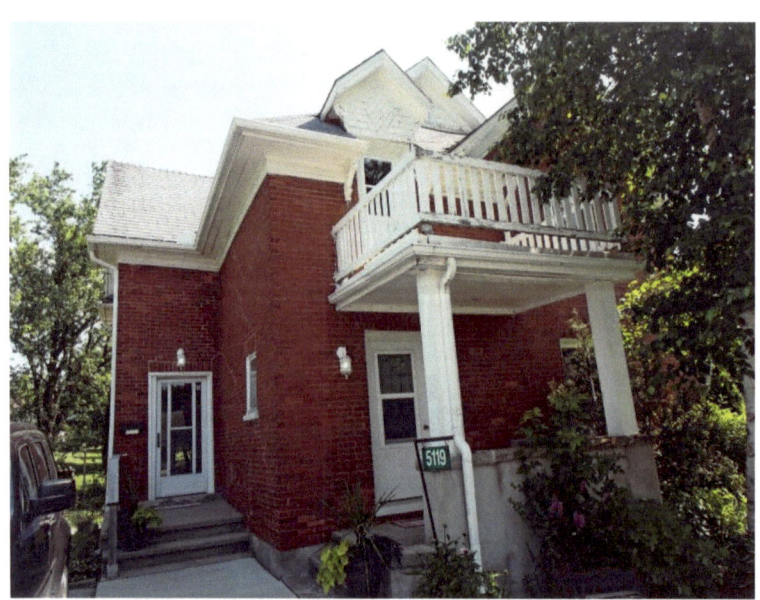

5119 Ament Line

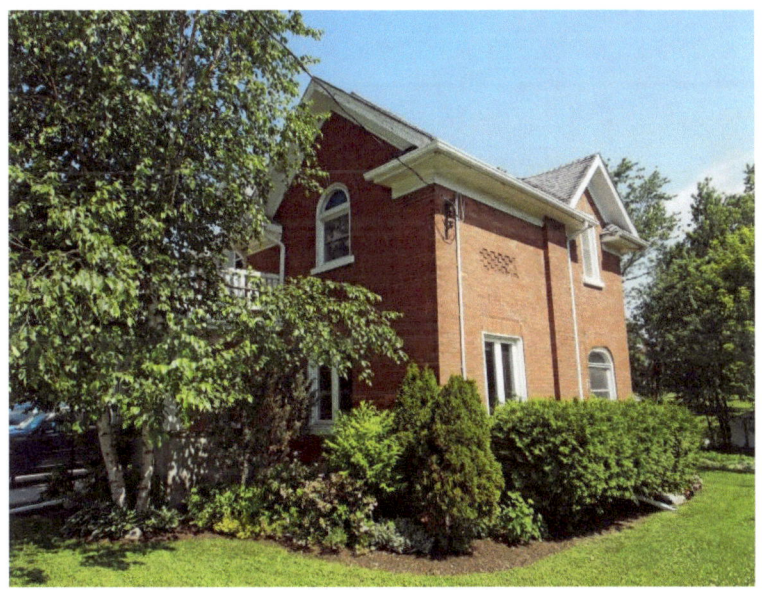

Ament Line

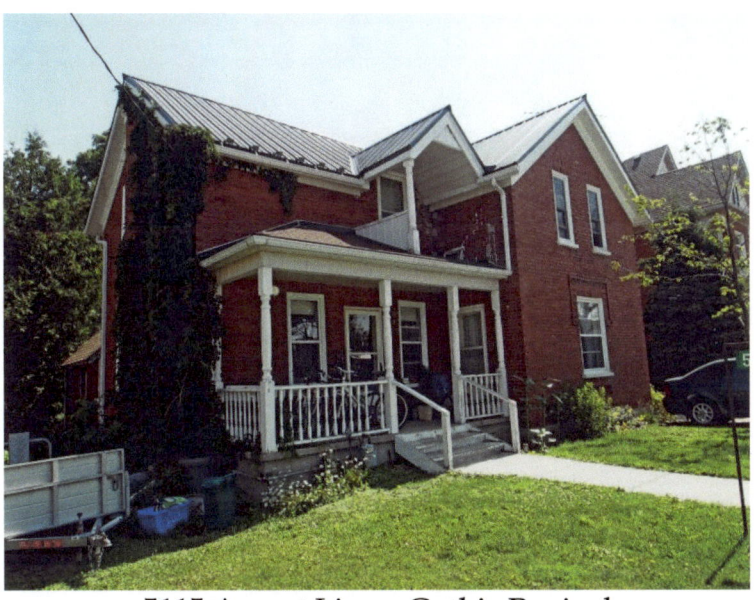

5115 Ament Line – Gothic Revival

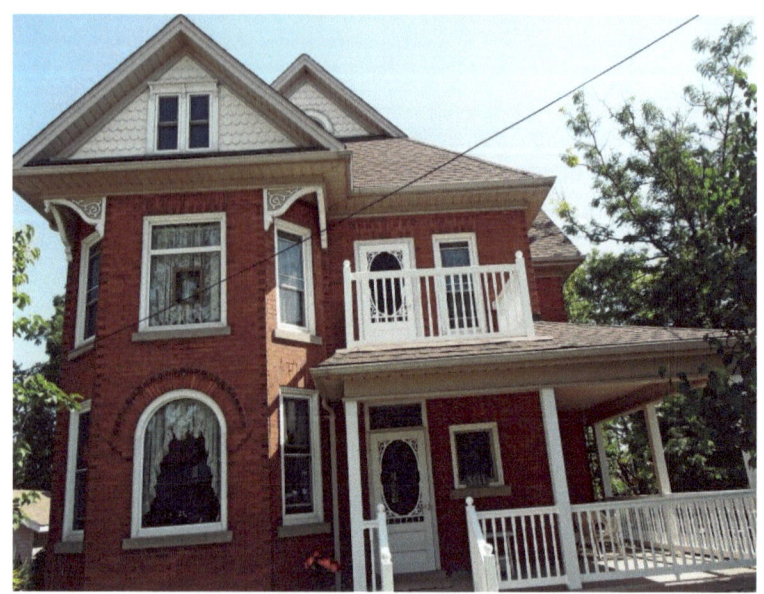

Ament Line – Edwardian, fretwork

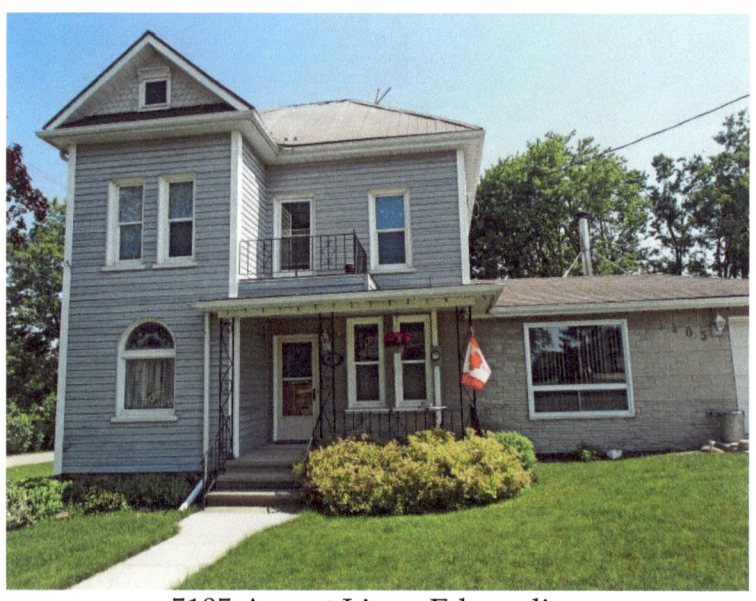

5105 Ament Line - Edwardian

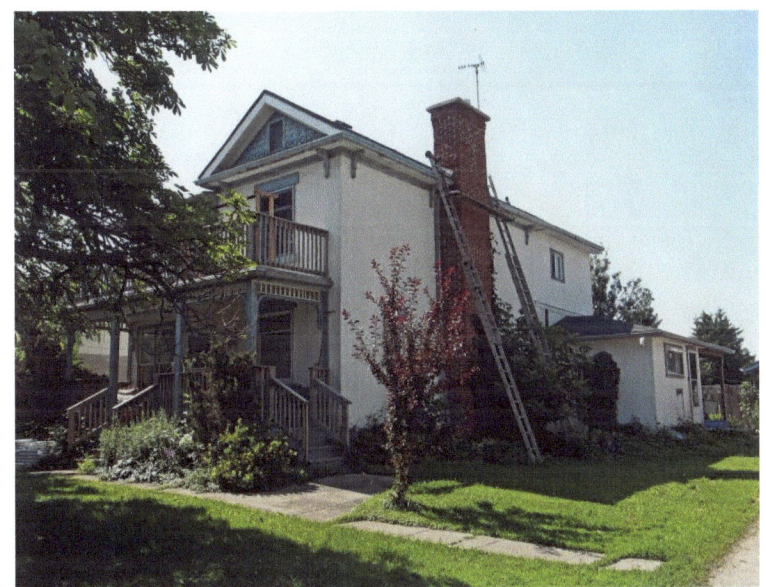

5102 Ament Line - Edwardian

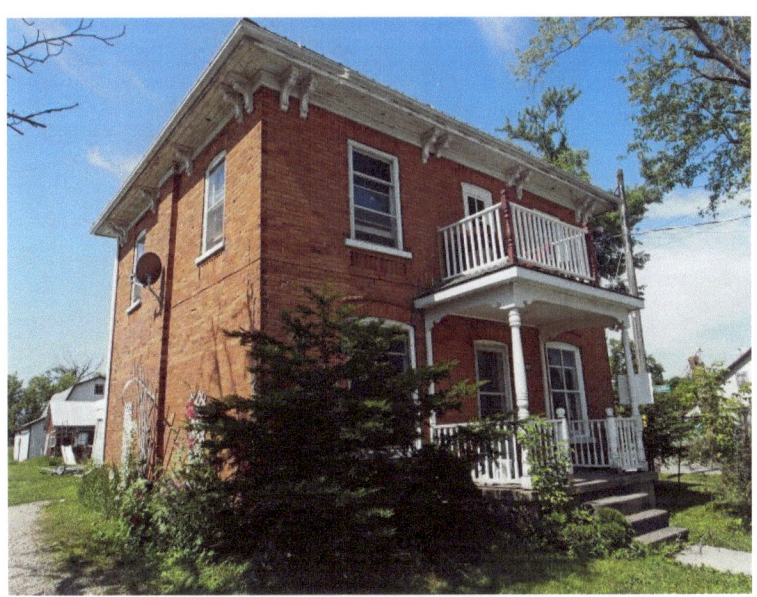

5106 Ament Line – Italianate, cornice brackets

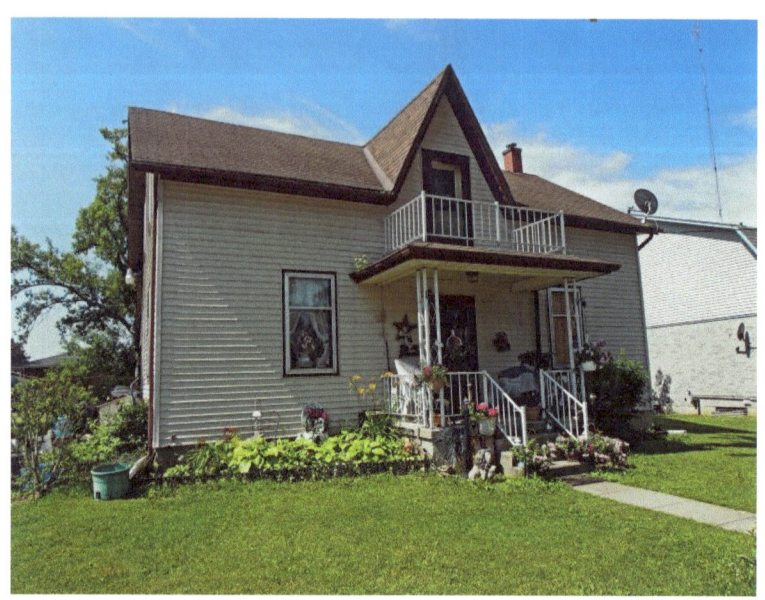

5112 Ament Line – Gothic Revival

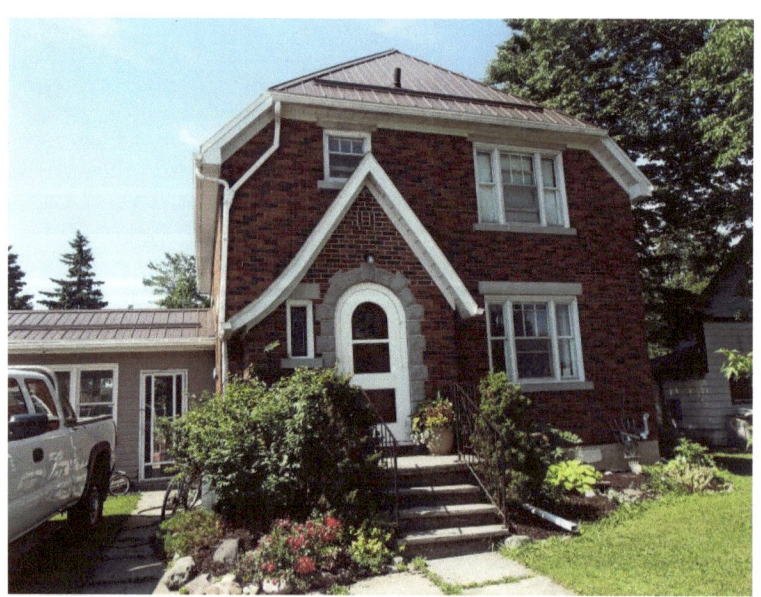

5120 Ament Line

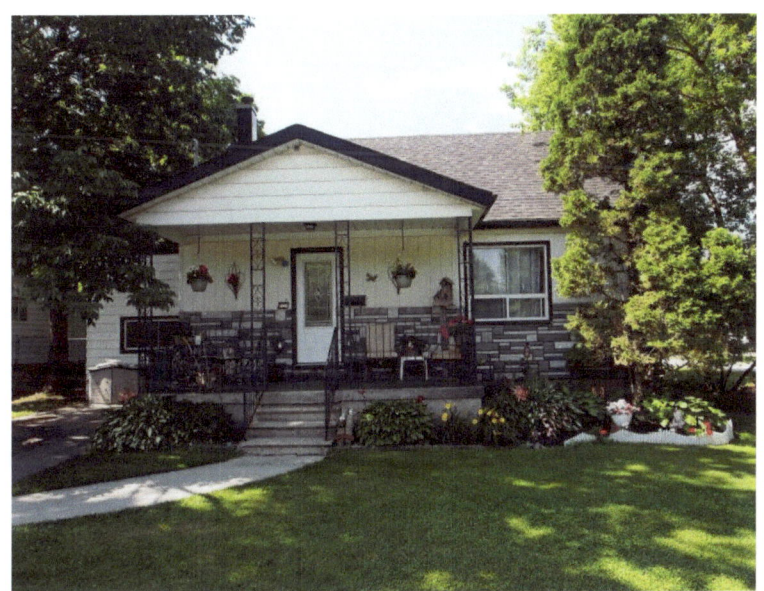

5124 Ament Line

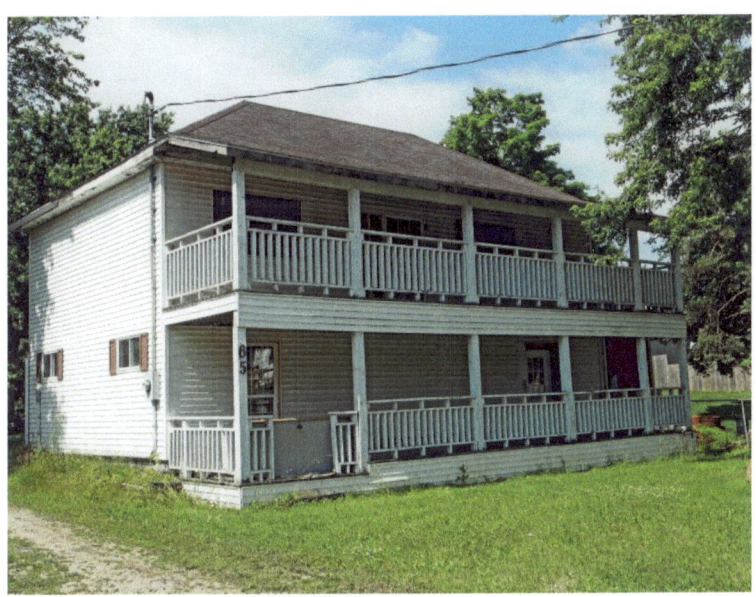

5142 Ament Line - Georgian

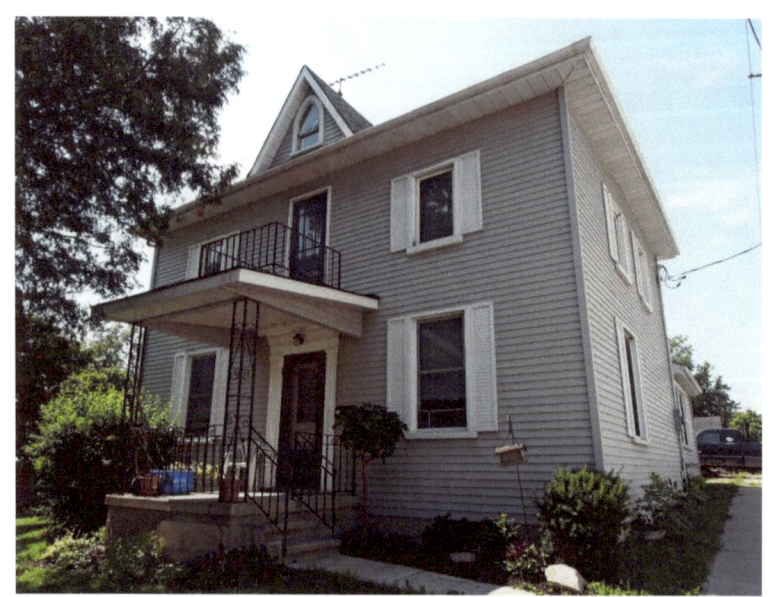

5148 Ament Line – Gothic Revival

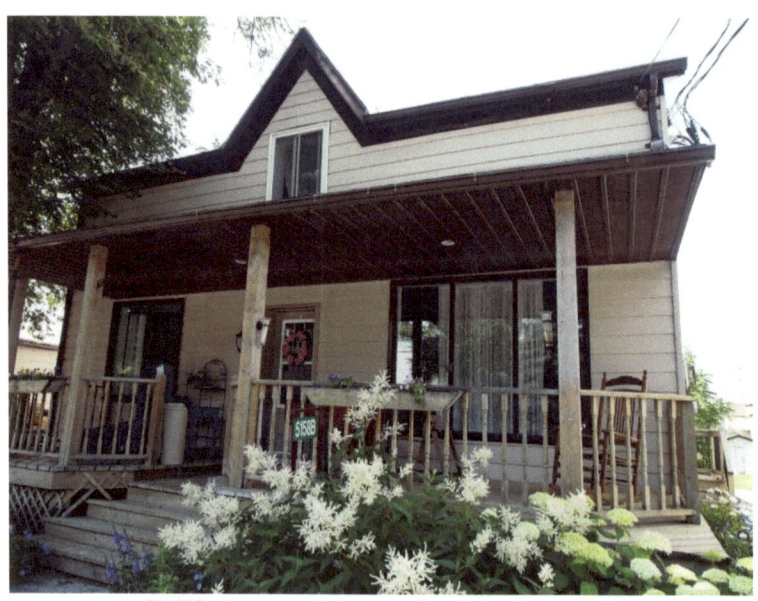

5158 Ament Line – Gothic Revival

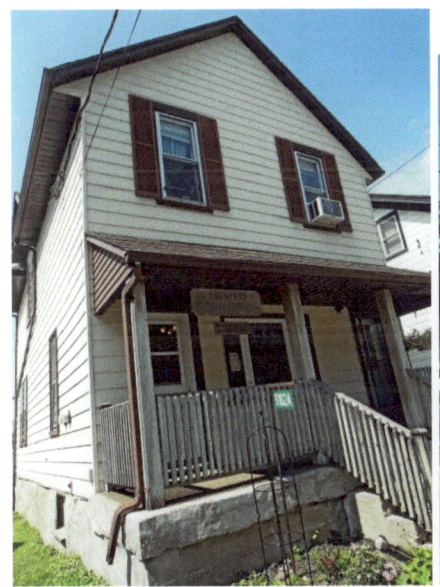
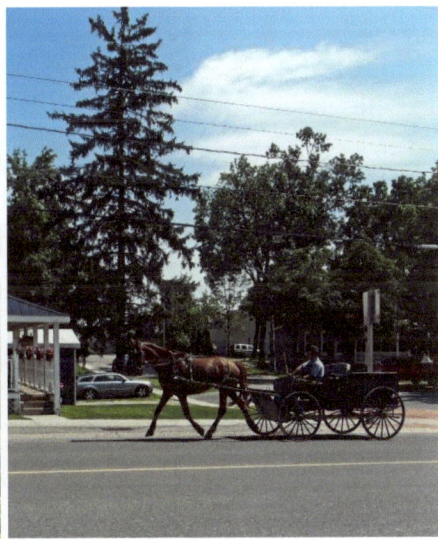

5162 Ament Line
Gothic Revival

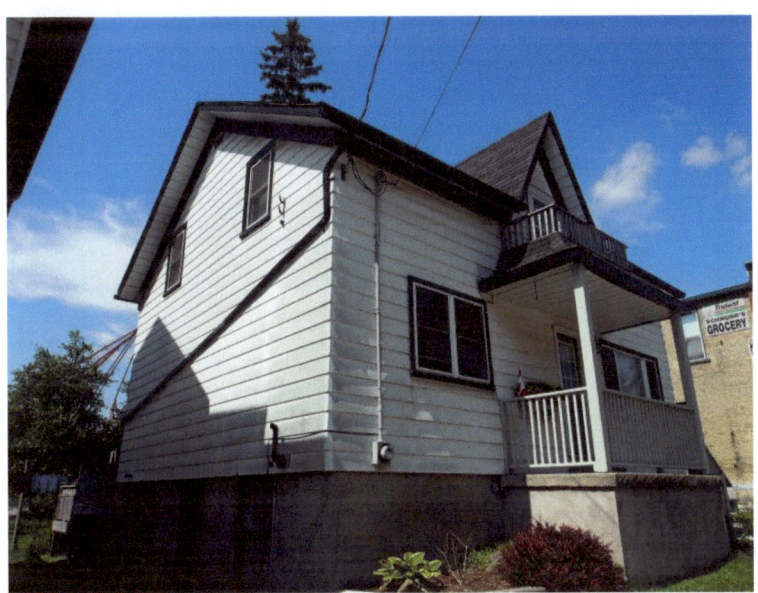

Ament Line – Gothic Revival

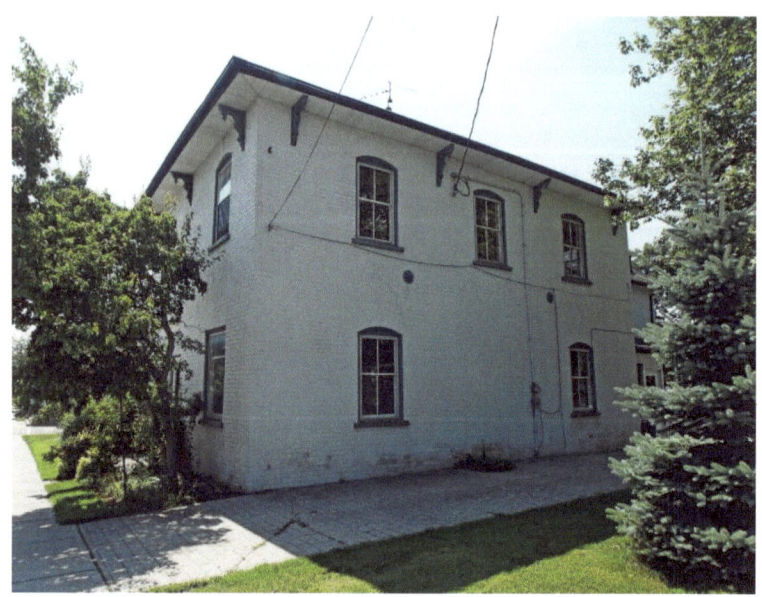

5176 Ament Line – Italianate – cornice brackets

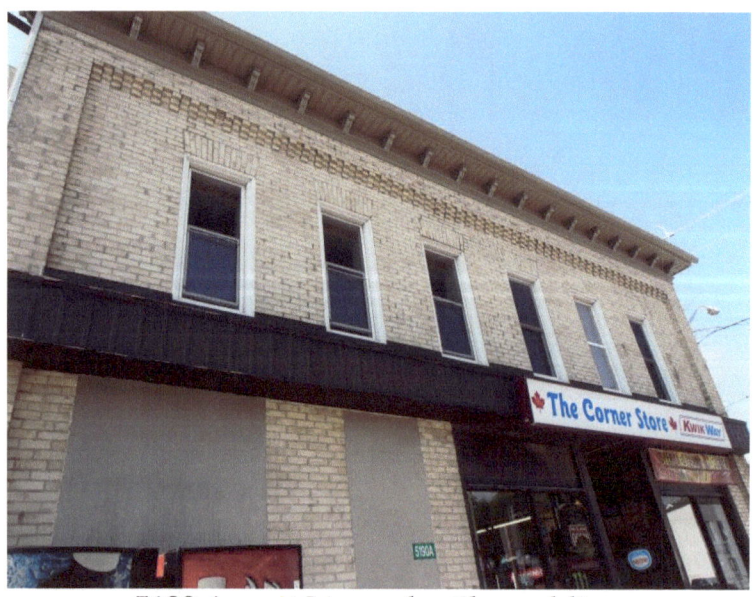

5190 Ament Line – dentil moulding

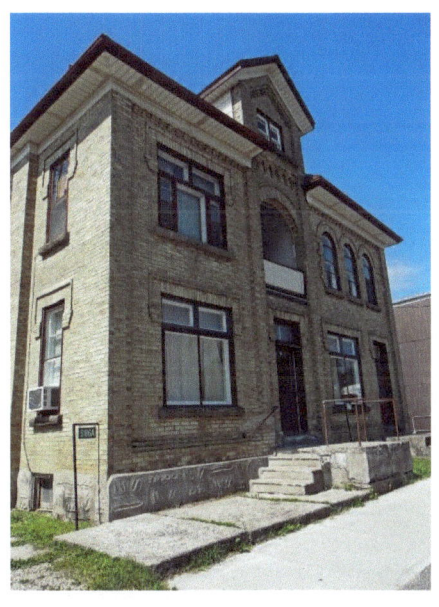

5186 Ament Line – Italianate, with two-and-a-half storey
tower-like structure, arched window voussoirs,
Dentil moulding

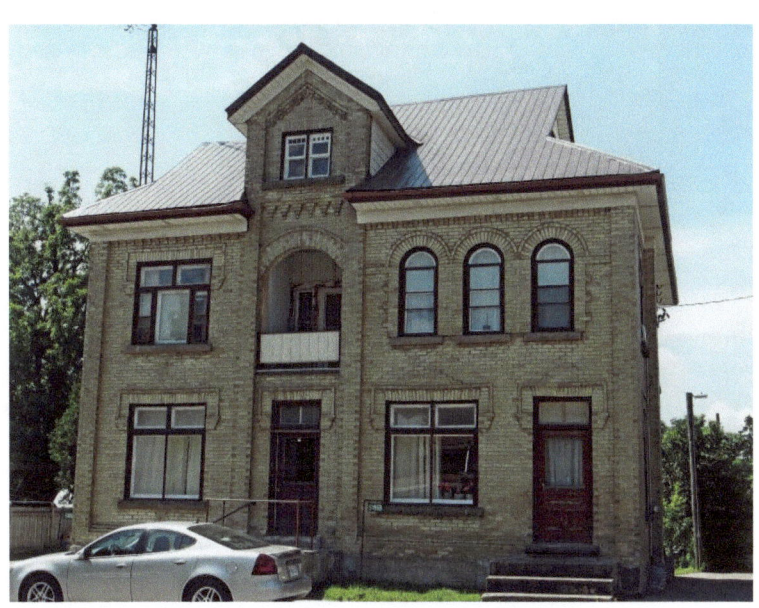

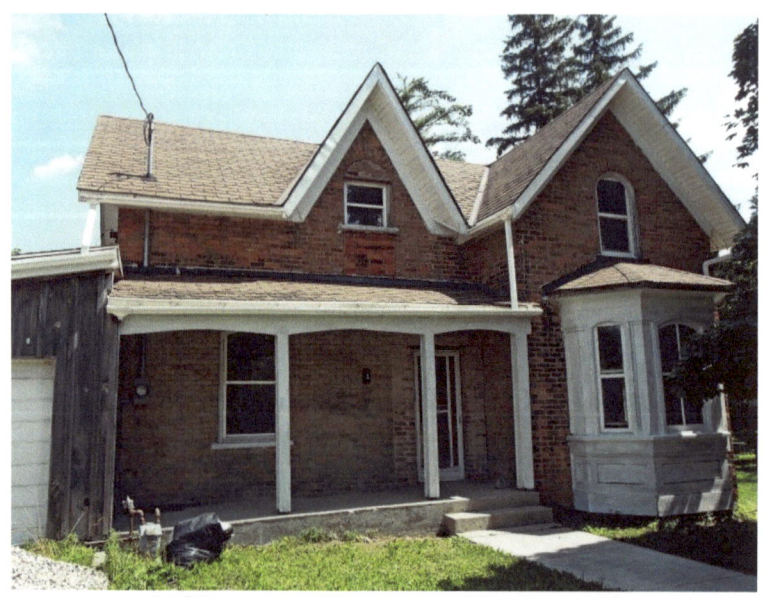

5185 Ament Line – Gothic Revival

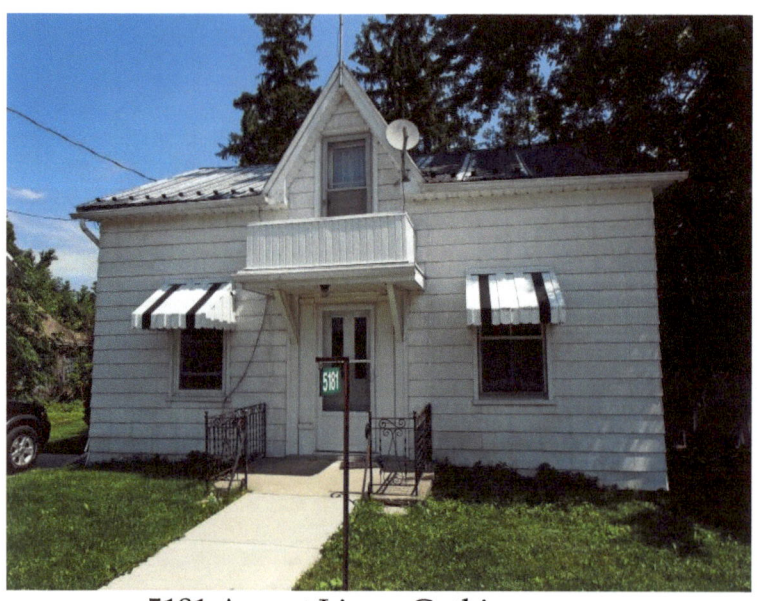

5181 Ament Line – Gothic cottage

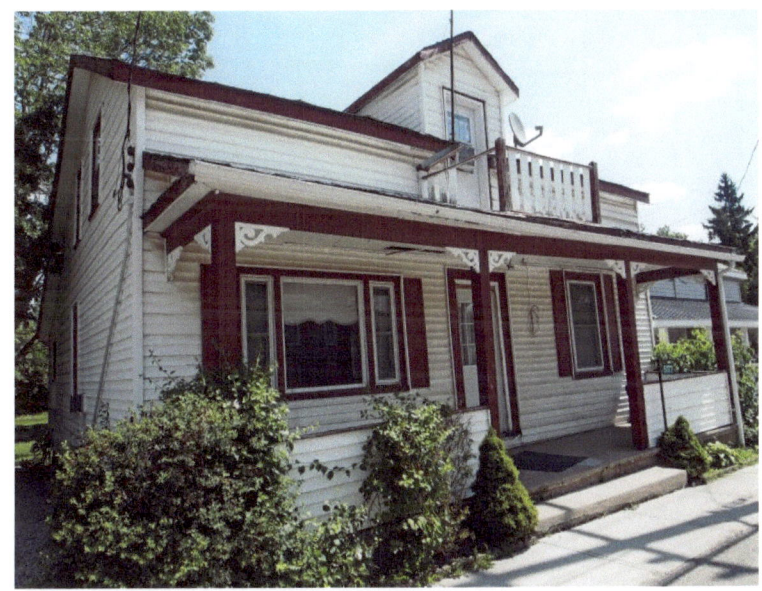

5177 Ament Line

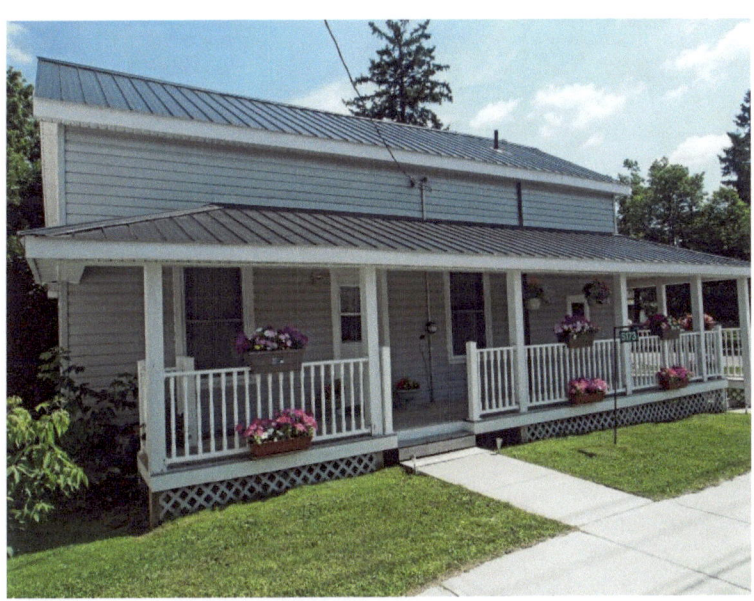

5173 Ament Line - Georgian

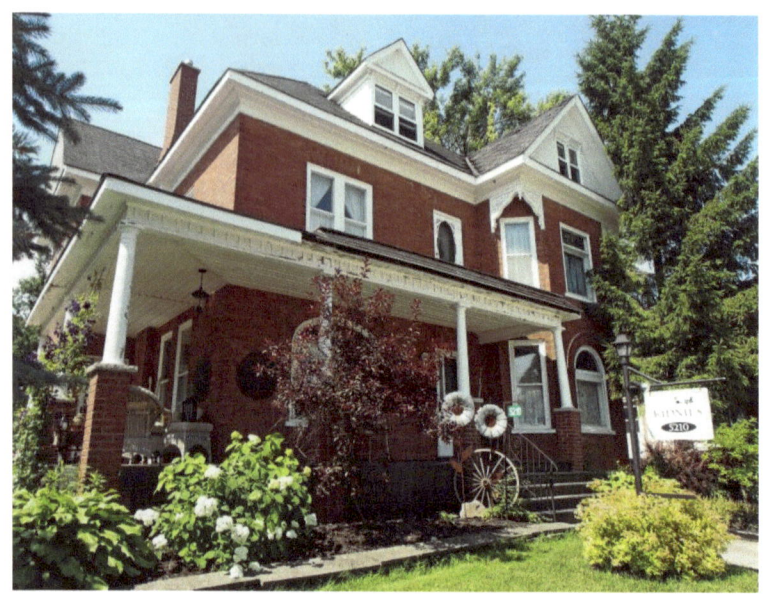

5210 Ament Line – Italianate with two-and-a-half storey
tower-like bay, fretwork, dormer in attic,
wrap-around verandah

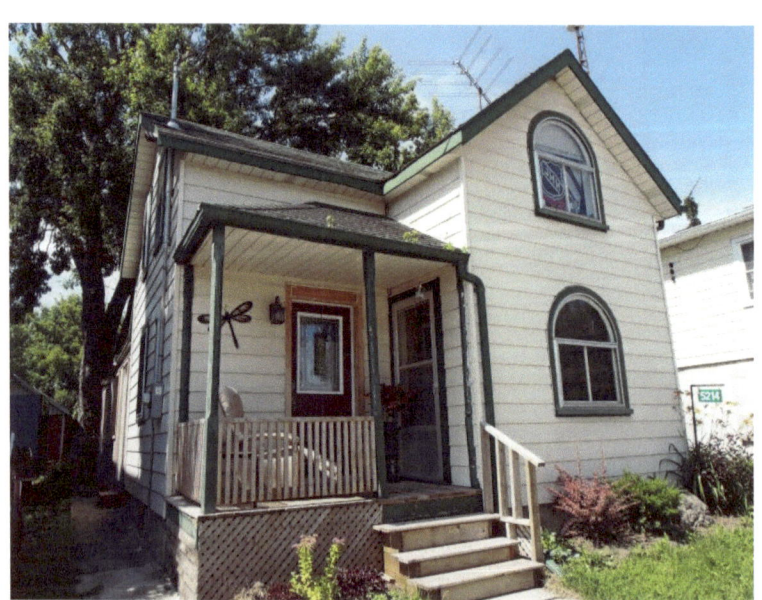

5214 Ament Line – Gothic Revival

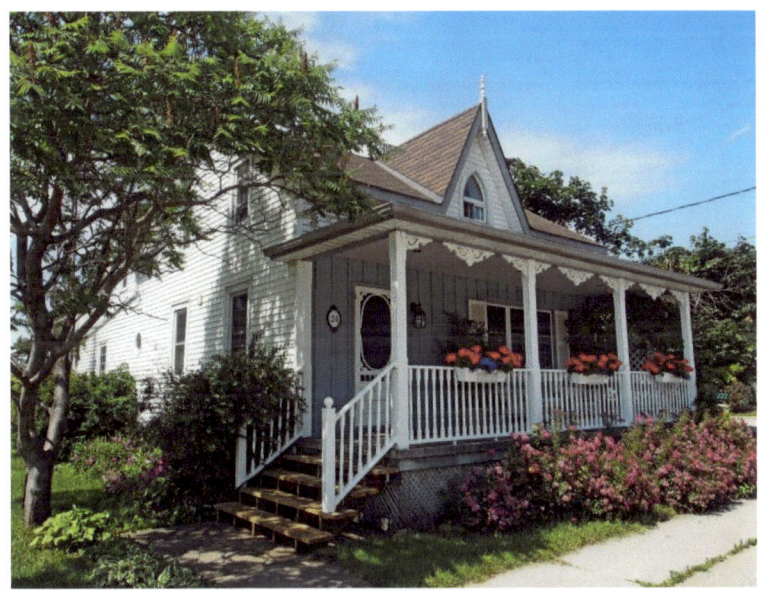

5222 Ament Line – Gothic Revival, finial on gable

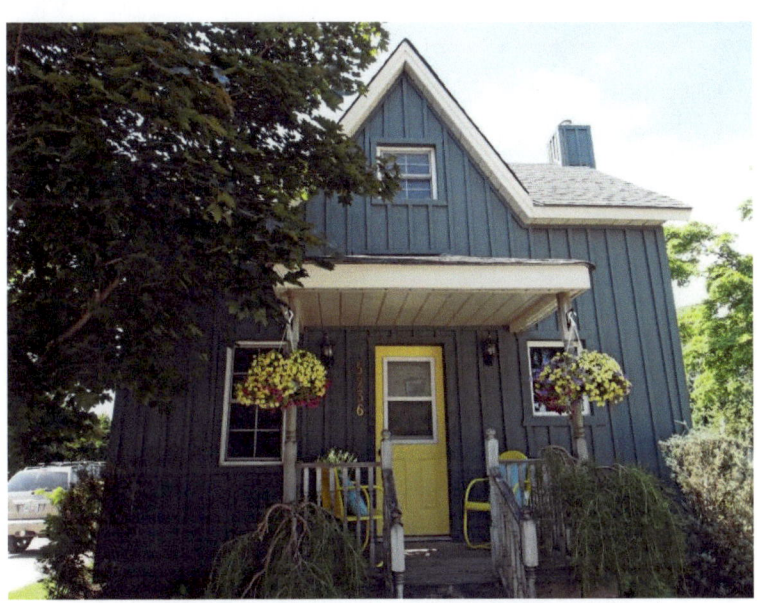

5236 Ament Line – Gothic Revival

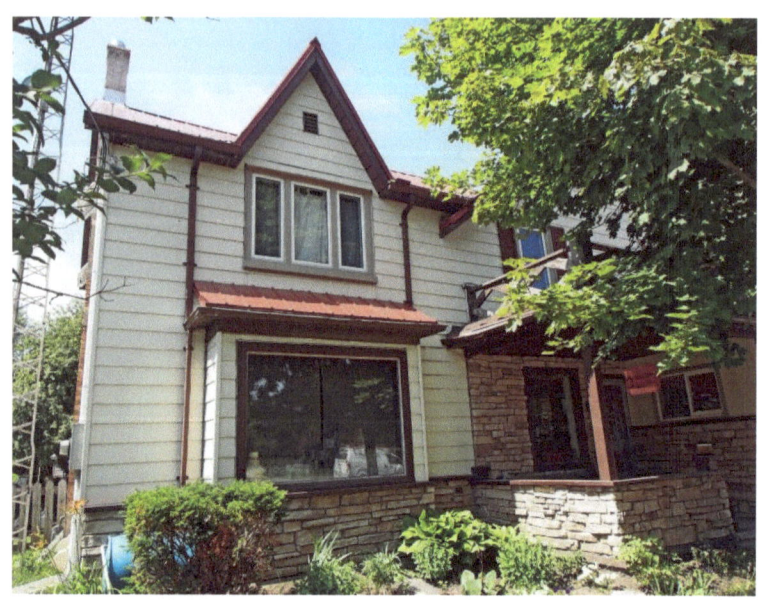

5248 Ament Line – Gothic Revival

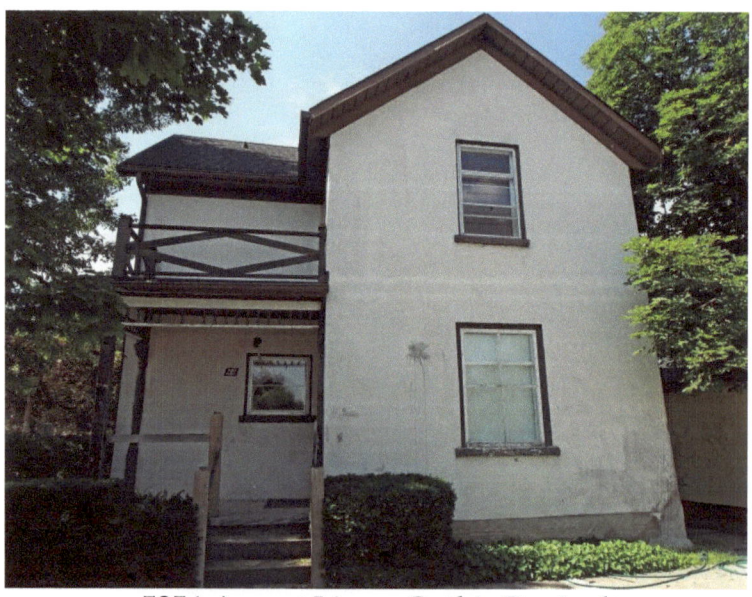

5254 Ament Line – Gothic Revival

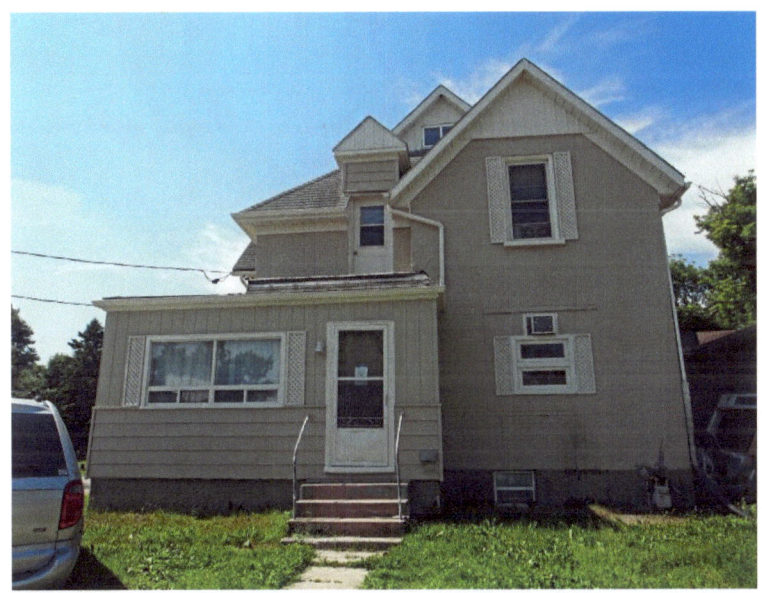

5288 Ament Line

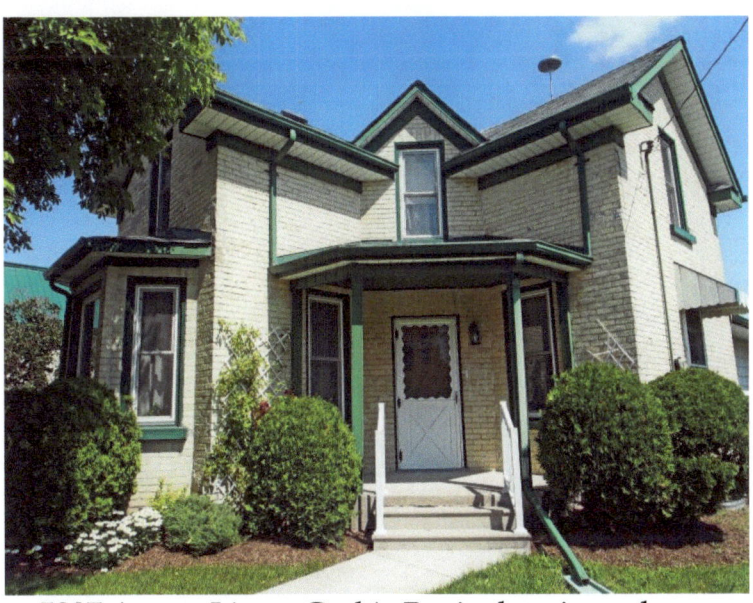

5297 Ament Line – Gothic Revival, unique shape,
cornice return on end gable

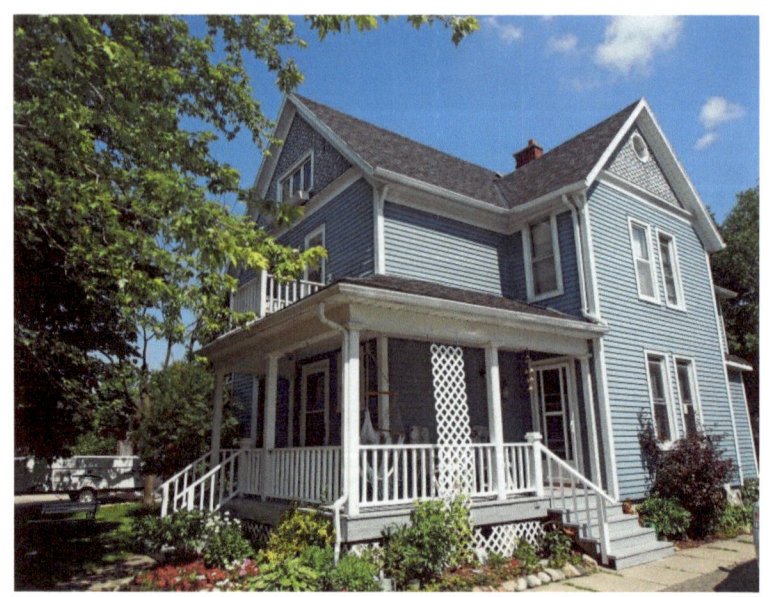

5245 Ament Line

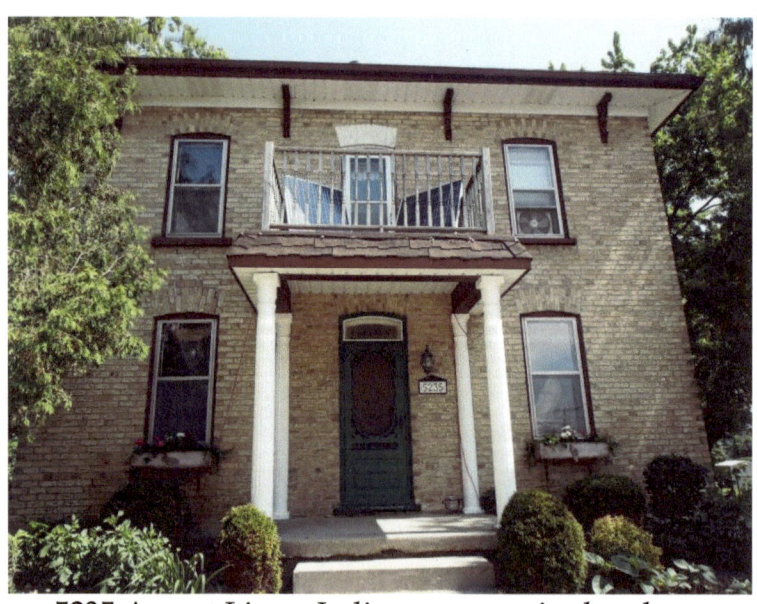

5235 Ament Line – Italianate – cornice brackets, balcony on second floor

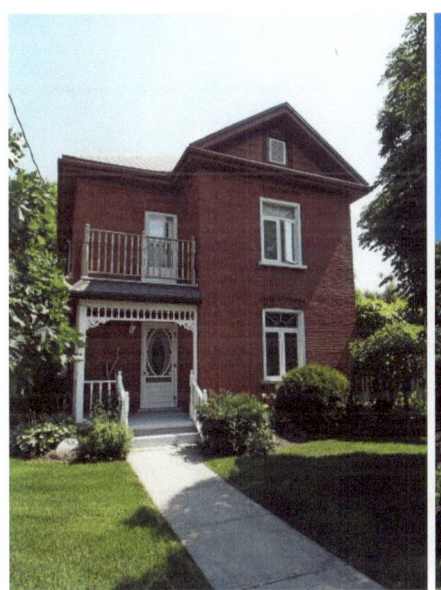

5221 Ament Line
Edwardian

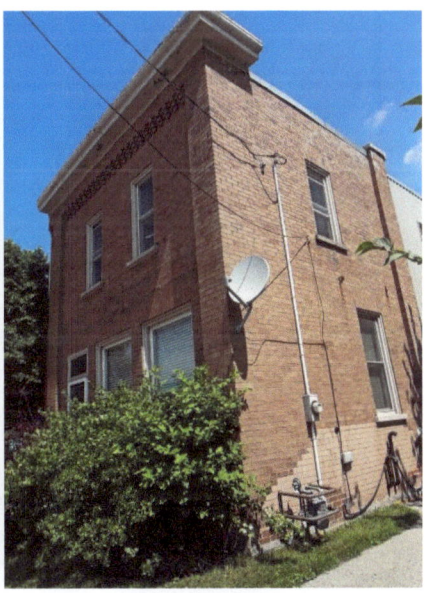

Ament Line
Italianate, dentil moulding

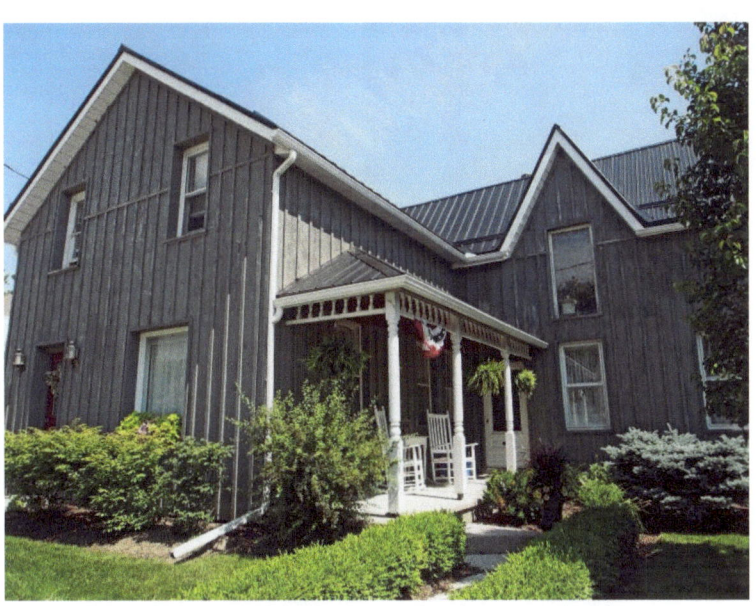

5215 Ament Line – Gothic Revival

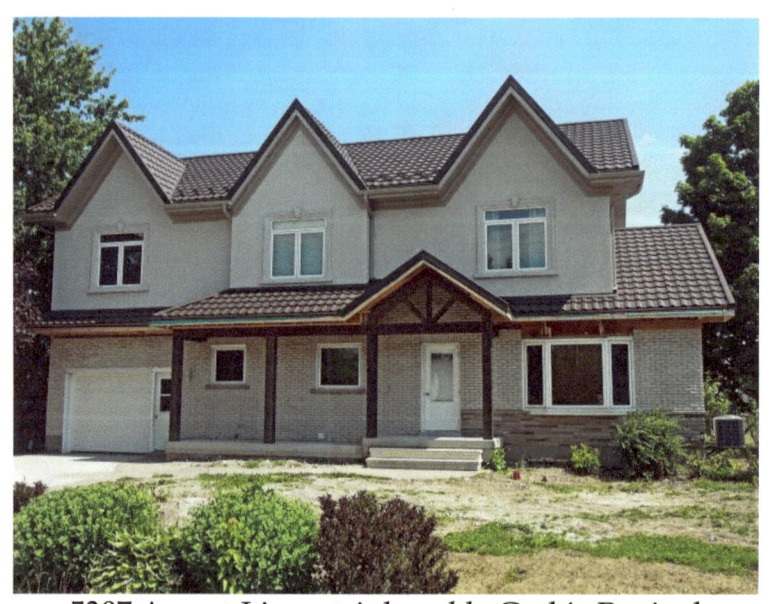

5307 Ament Line – triple gable Gothic Revival

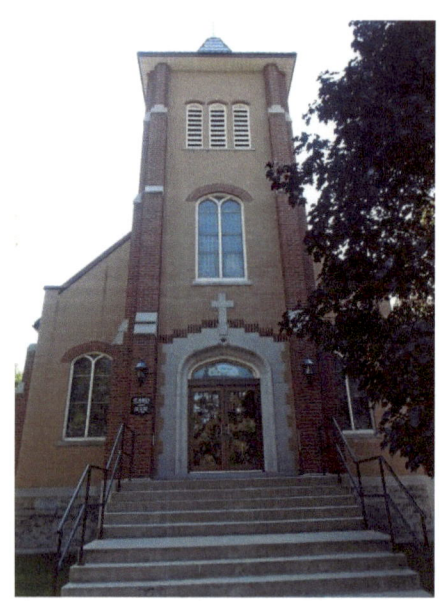

St. Mary's Catholic Church 1043 Isabella Street

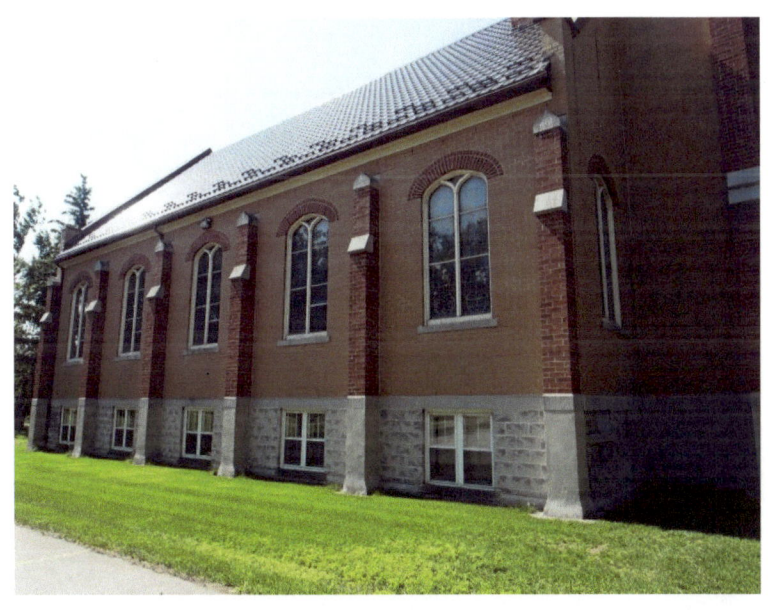

St. Mary's Catholic Church

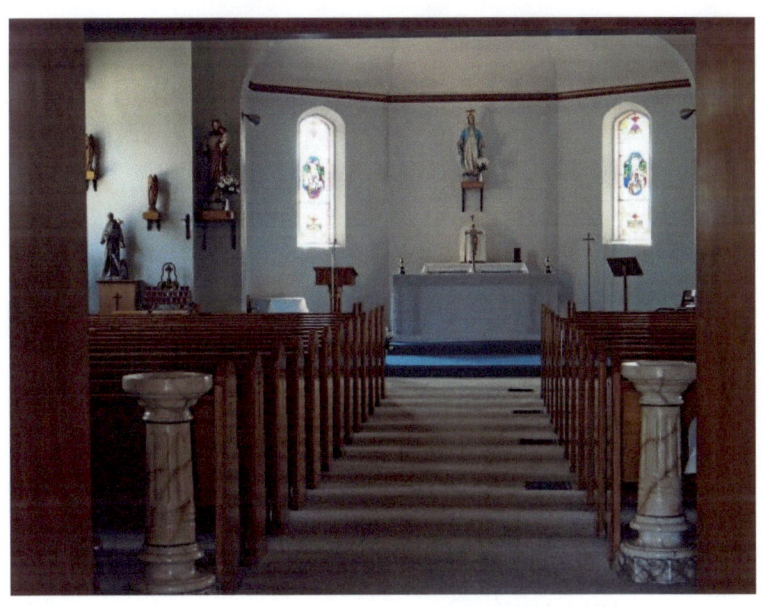

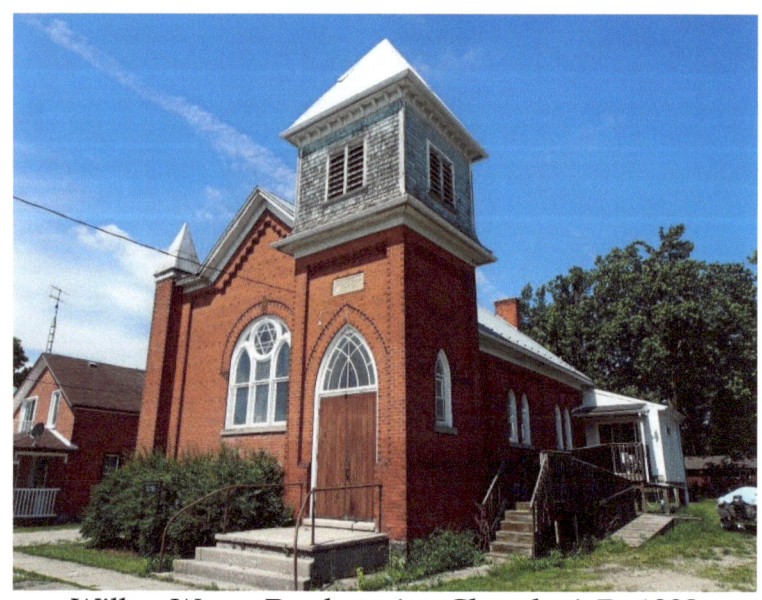

Wilker Way – Presbyterian Church A.D. 1908

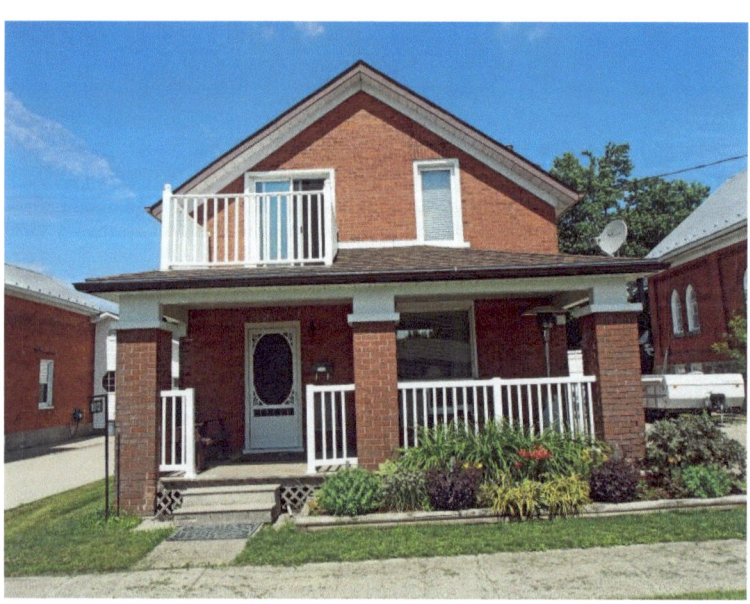

1012 Wilker Way – Gothic Revival

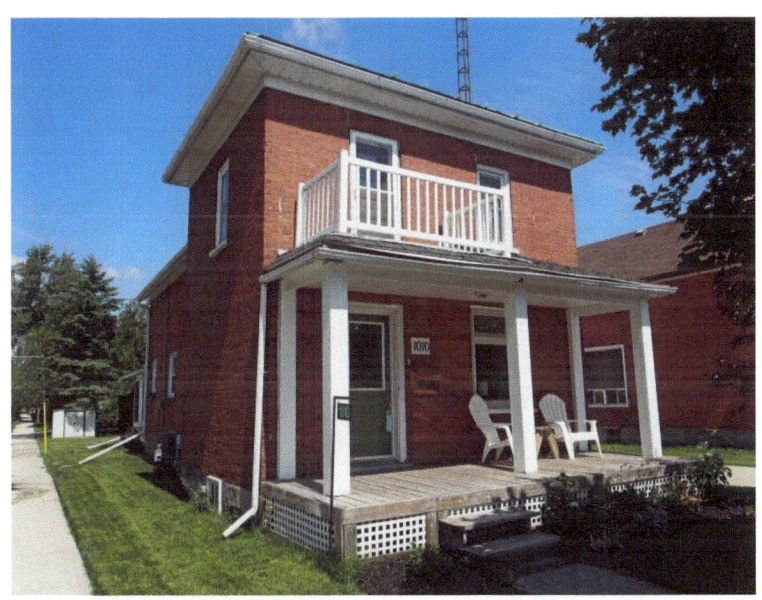

1010 Wilker Way – Italianate – hipped roof, balcony on second floor

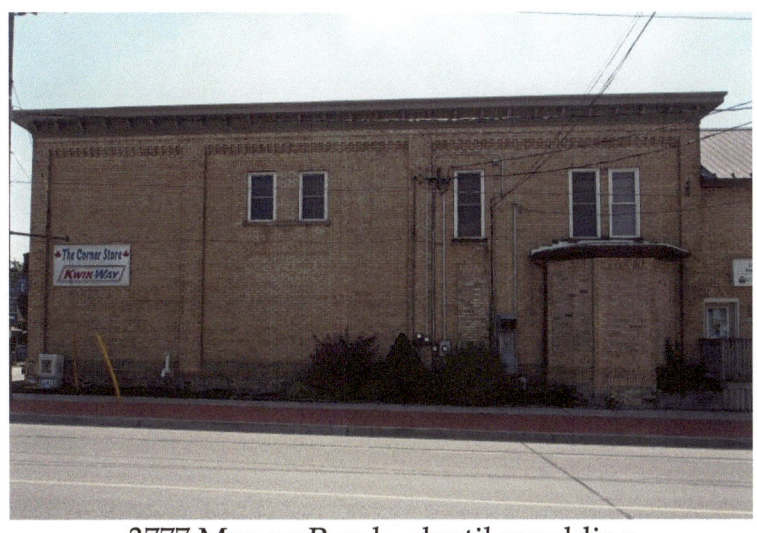

3777 Manser Road – dentil moulding

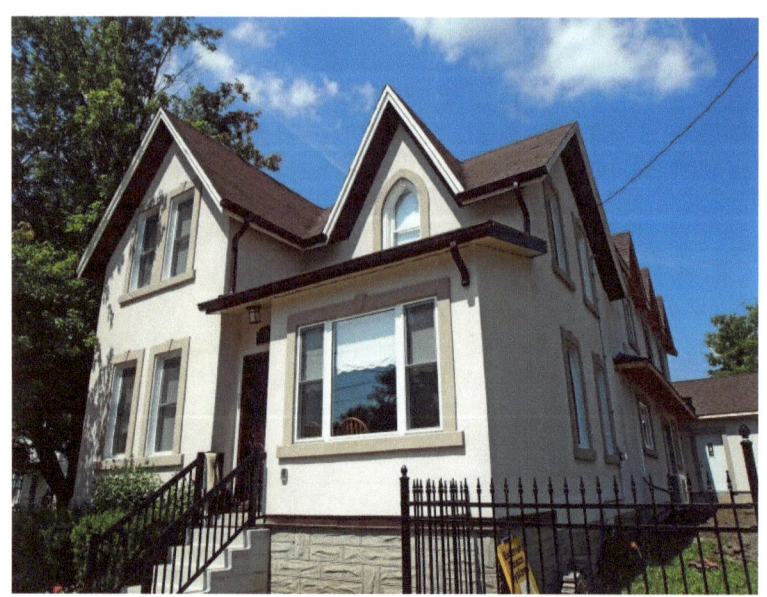

3744 Manser Road – Gothic Revival

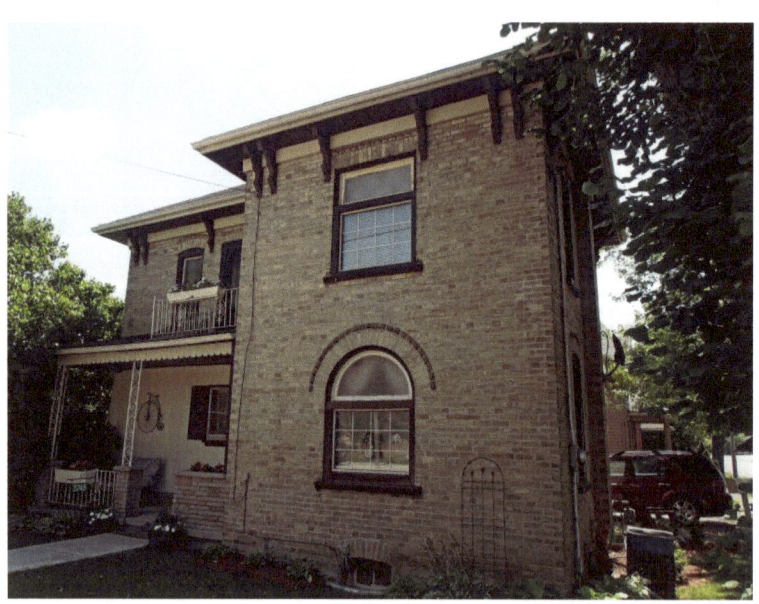

3745 Manser Road – Italianate, cornice brackets,
Romanesque style window arch

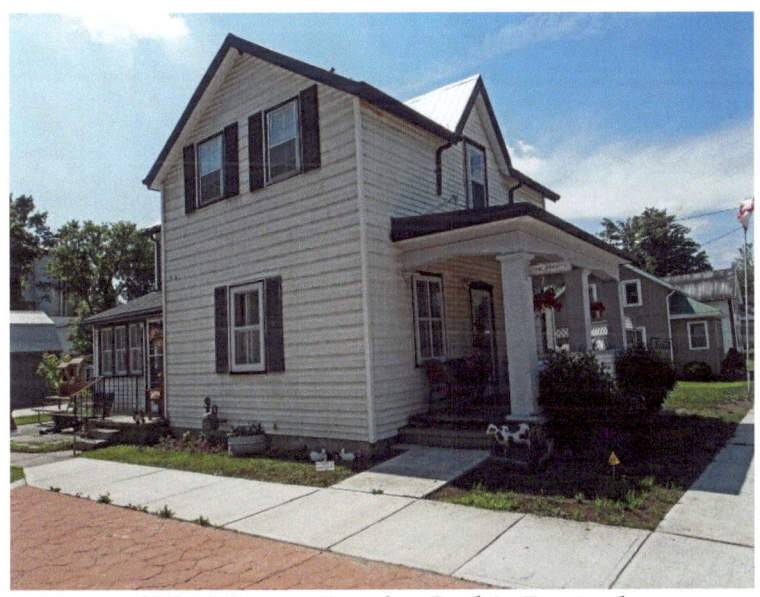

3731 Manser Road – Gothic Revival

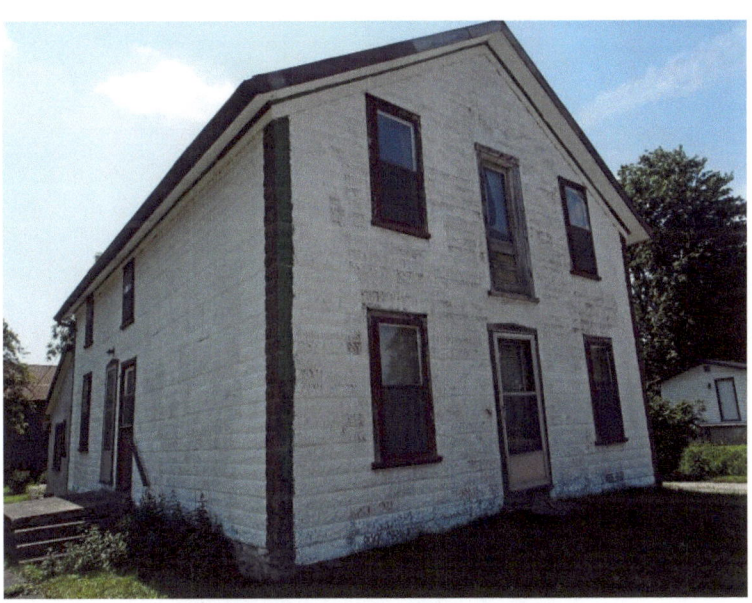

3719 Manser Road - Gothic

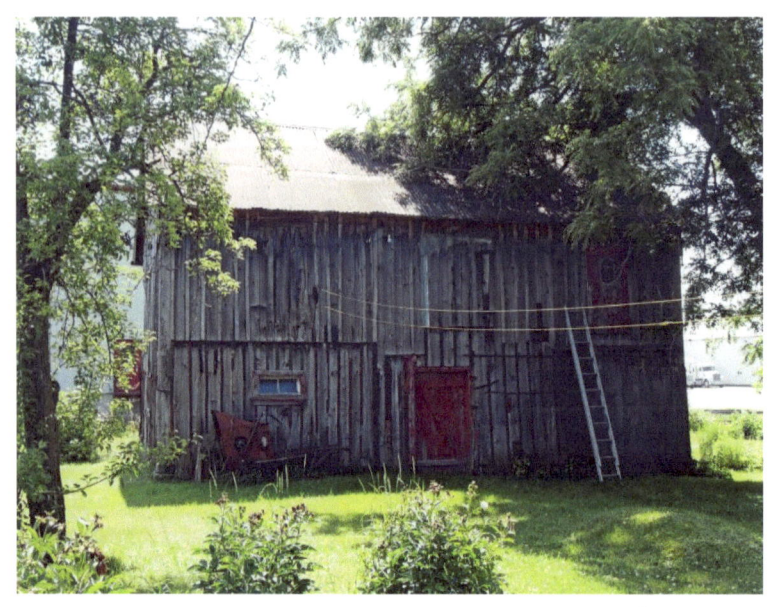

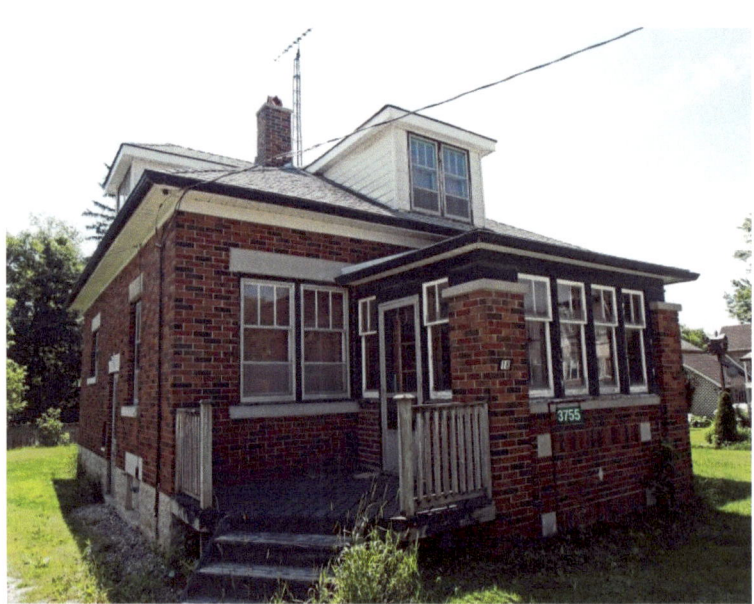

3755 Manser Road – Italianate, hipped roof, dormers

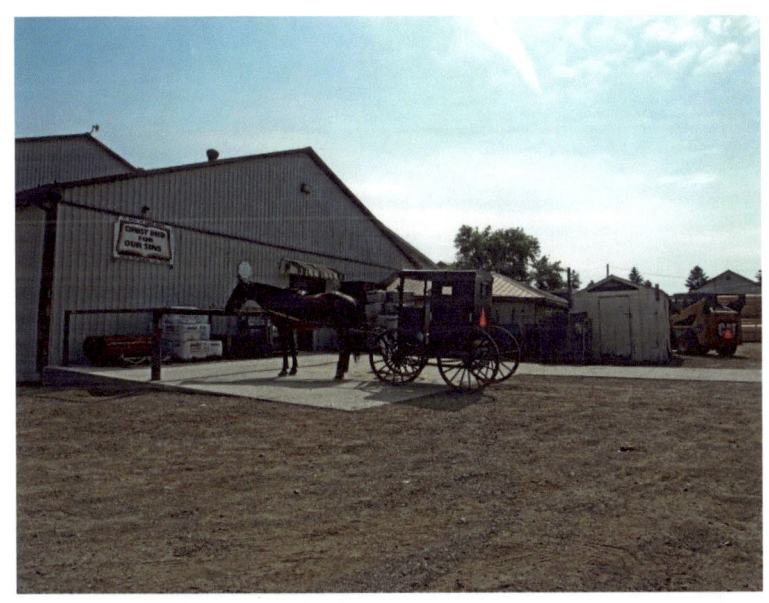

Macton

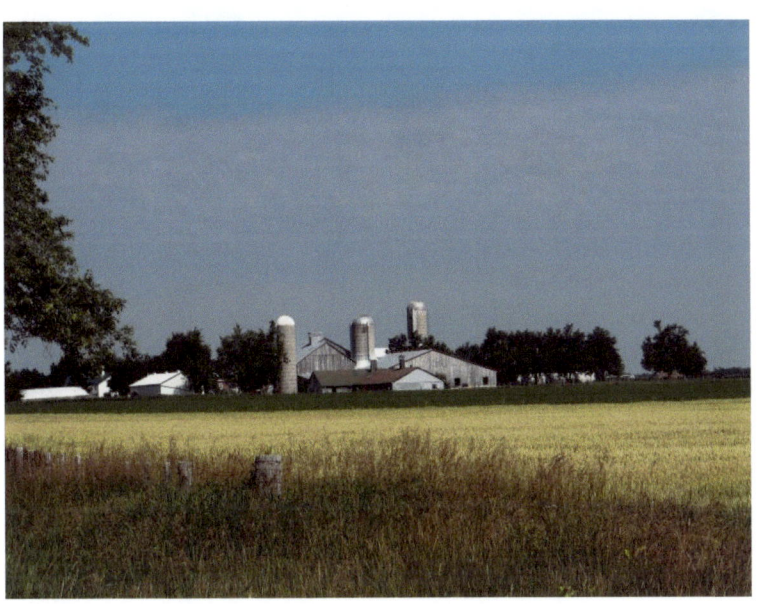

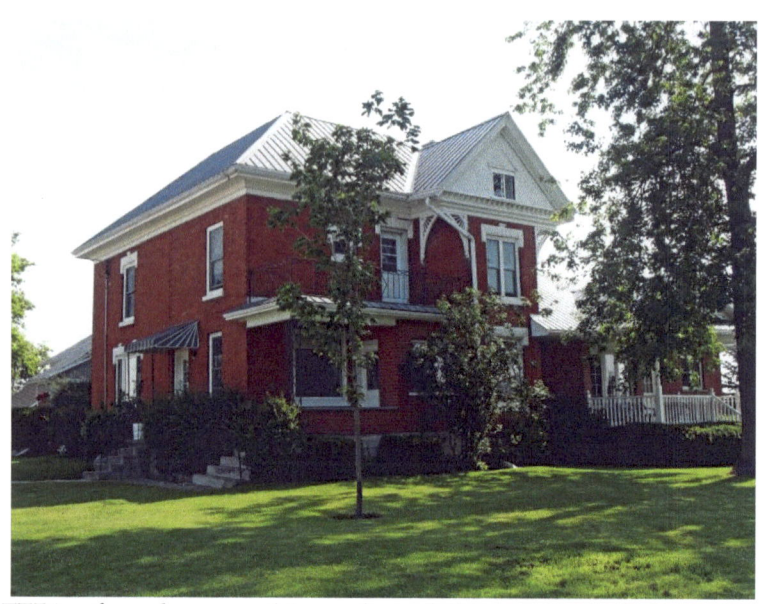

#7751 – farmhouse – hipped roof, fretwork, Italianate with two-and-a-half storey tower-like bay

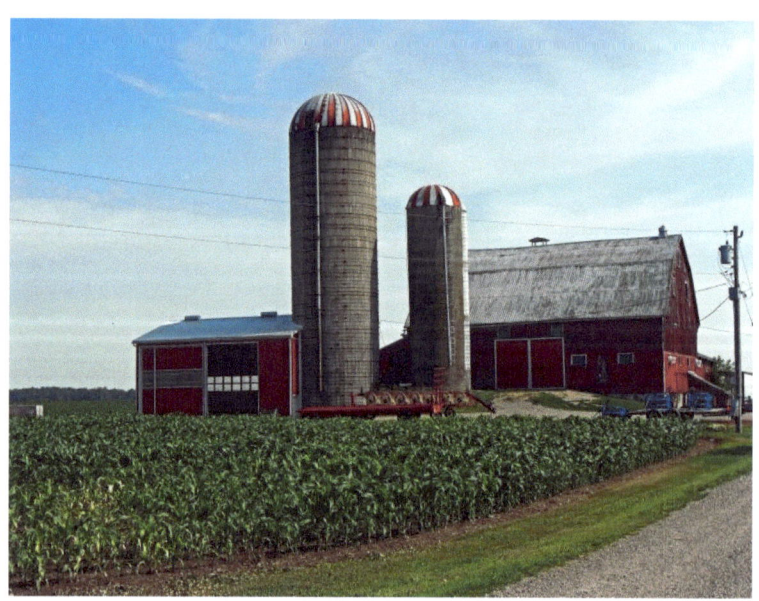

#7751 – barn

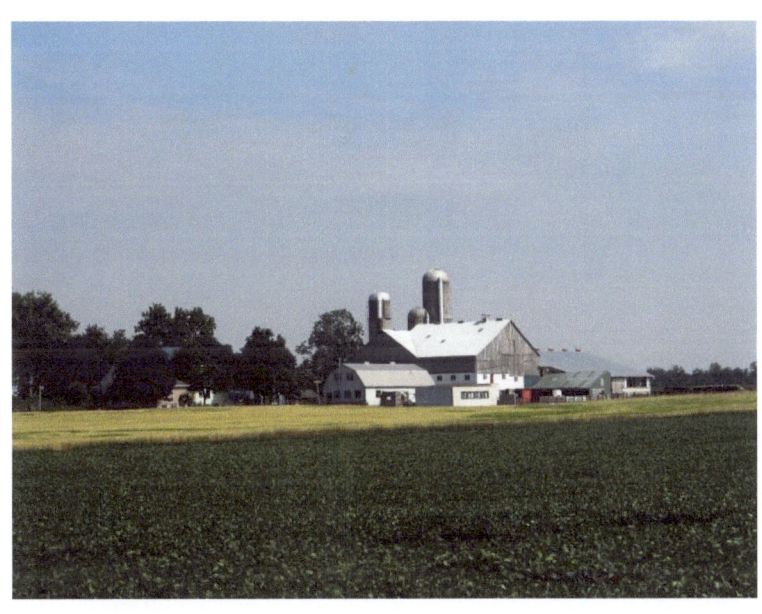

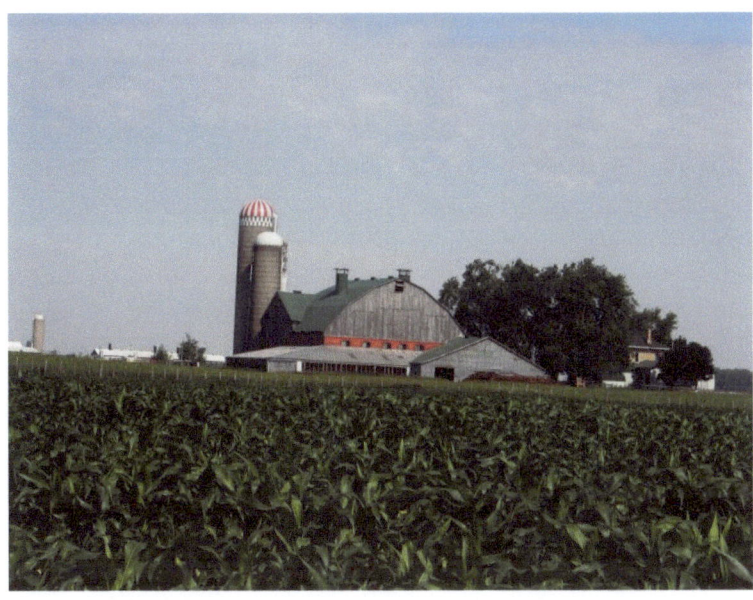

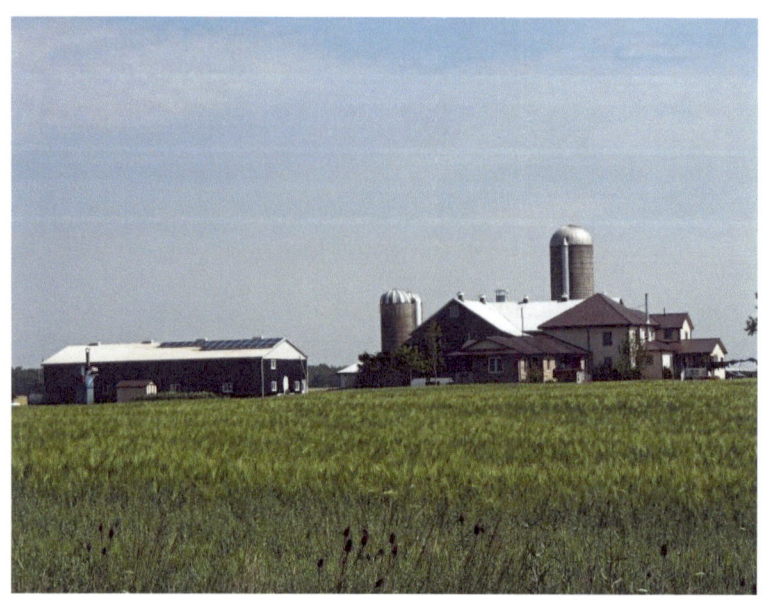

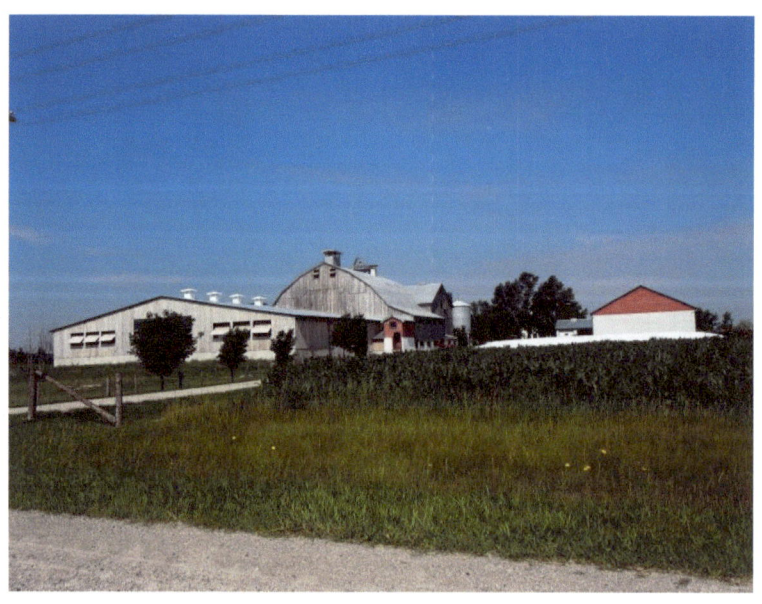

Erbsville

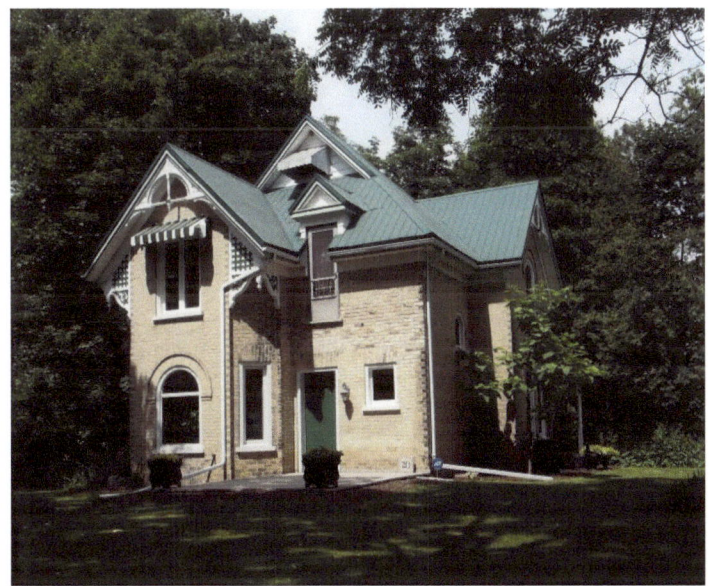

Queen Anne style, Vergeboard trim on gables

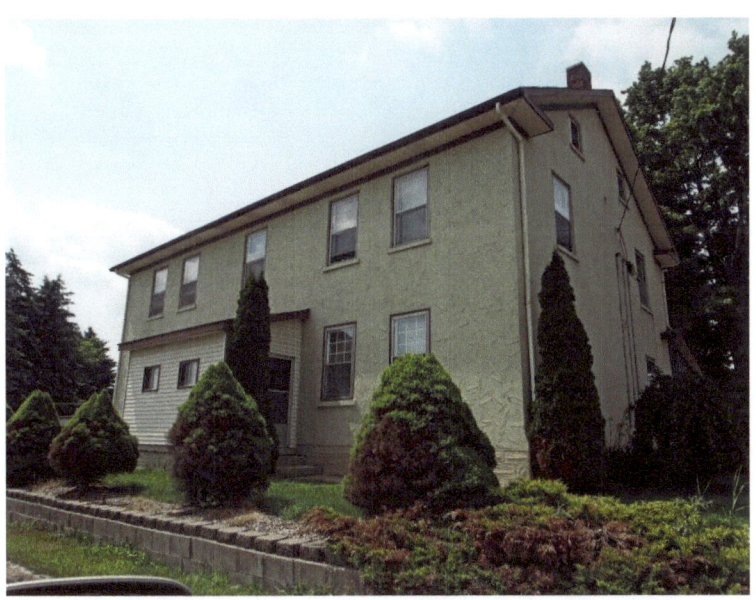

Georgian style, cornice return on end gable

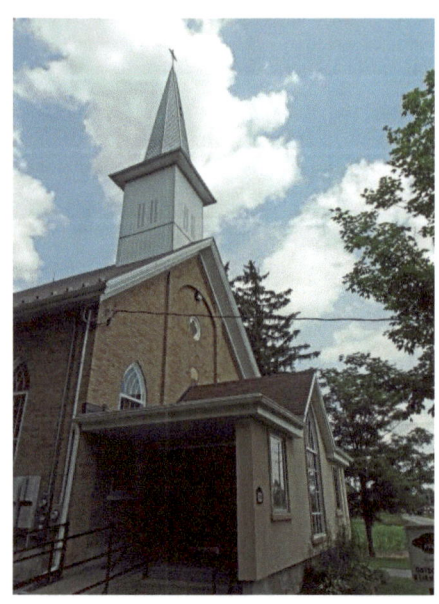

c. 1877

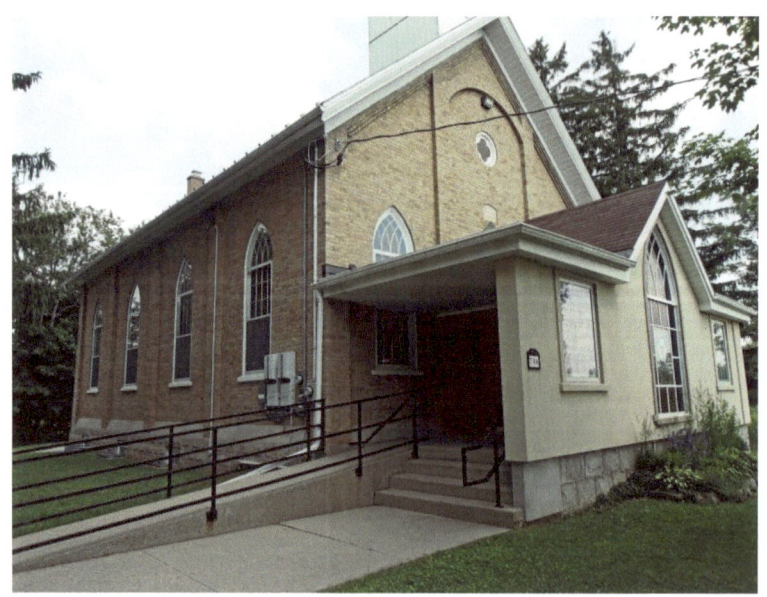

Gothic style, lancet windows

Architectural Terms

Brackets: a decorative or weight-bearing structural element which forms a right angle with one side against a wall and the other under a projecting surface such as an eave or roof. Example: Ament Line, Linwood	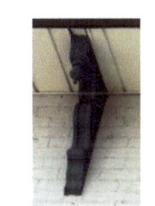
Cornice: originally the wooden overhang of the roof. With the use of stone, brick, iron and steel, the cornice is any projecting shelf at the top of a ceiling or roof. They can be very decorative. Example: 1029 Ament Line, Linwood	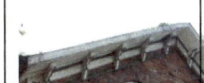
Cornice Return: decorative element on the end of a gable. Example: 5297 Ament Line, Linwood	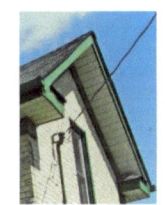
Dentil Moulding: an even series of rectangles used as ornamental decoration in cornices. Example: 5168 Ament Line, Linwood	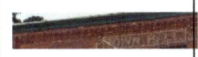
Dichromatic brickwork: the use of two colours of brick, tile or slate to decorate a façade. Example: Macton Church	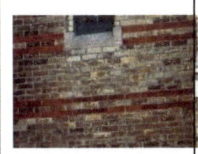

Dormer: (French for "sleep") a gable end window that pierces through the plane of a sloping roof surface to create usable space in the top floor or attic of a building by adding headroom. Example: 1030 Ament Line, Linwood	
Finial: ornament added to the top of a gable, pinnacle, canopy or spire – a Gothic element. Example: 5222 Ament Line, Linwood	
Fretwork: interlaced decorative design resembling a bracket Example: Ament Line, Linwood	
Gable: the triangular portion of a wall between the edges of a sloping roof. Example: 5158 Ament Line, Linwood	
Hipped Roof: a roof where all sides slope downwards to the walls with no gables. Example: Macton - farmhouse	

Lancet Window: a tall, narrow window with a pointed arch at its top. Example: Macton Church	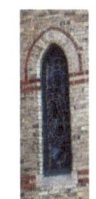
Vergeboard: also called bargeboards – hang from the projecting end of a roof and are often elaborately carved and ornamented. Example: Erbsville	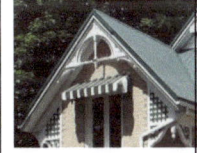

Building Styles

Edwardian, 1900-1930 – This style bridges the ornate and elaborate styles of the Victorian era and the simplified styles of the 20th century. Balanced facades, simple roof lines, dormer windows, large front porches, and smooth brick surfaces are its characteristics. Example: Ament Line, Linwood	
Georgian, before 1860 – This style began with the British King Georges in the 18th century. These buildings have balanced facades around a central door, medium-pitched gable roofs, and small paned windows. Example: 5142 Ament Line, Linwood	
Gothic Revival, 1830-1890 – These decorative buildings have sharply-pitched gables with highly detailed vergeboards, pointed-arch window openings, and dichromatic brickwork. It is a common style in Ontario. Example: 5185 Ament Line, Linwood	
Italianate, 1850-1900 – It has wide-bracketed eaves, belvederes, wrap-around verandahs. Example: 5106 Ament Line, Linwood	
Queen Anne, 1885-1900 – This style is distinguished by an irregular outline featuring a combination of an offset tower, broad gables, projecting two-storey bays, verandahs, multi-sloped roofs, and tall, decorative chimneys. A mixture of brick and wood is common. Windows often have one large single-paned bottom sash and small panes in the upper sash. Example: Erbsville	

www.ingramcontent.com/pod-product-compliance
Lightning Source LLC
Chambersburg PA
CBHW040925180526
45159CB00002BA/609